Building Bridges: Understanding the Religions of Others

Buddhism, Christianity, Hinduism and Islam

ANTONY FERNANDO, ThD, PhD

Foreword by MARCUS BRAYBROOKE
Joint-President of the "World Congress of Faiths

All rights reserved. Copyright © 2018 Antony Fernando, ThD, PhD

No part of this book may be reproduced in any way without the express written permission of the publisher. First Published 2015 under the title: "Main Religions of the Modern World" and the "Two Forms of Any Religion".

The views, opinions, and research expressed in this website/book are those of the authors and do not necessarily reflect the position of iPub Global Connection LLC.

Cover Design by Arewa Abiodun Ibrahim

Photo Credit: "Japanese Garden" by Dean Hochman is licensed under CC by 2.0 https://www.flickr.com/photos/deanhochman/14757642237/shutterstock.com

ISBN: 978-1-948575-06-5
ISBN Kindle: 978-1-948575-07-2

In this book, the eight pictures of Hindu gods and goddesses were reproduced from an Indian book on Hinduism, or from the book "Hindu Gods and Goddesses" by Swami Harshananda published by Sri Ramakrishna Math, Mylapore, Madras, 600 004 India. The publication date was not published, the Foreword is dated 1981.

The picture on the postures of worship given in the section on Islam, were adopted from the book "Manner of Performing Prayers (For the beginners)" by Abdul Basil Quraishi, P.O.Box 83, Dharan Airport 31938. Publisher and publication date not given. All the other pictures are compositions of Antony Fernando.

About Antony Fernando

The author has a doctorate in Theology (Rome), a doctorate in Buddhist Culture (Lanka) and a Higher Diploma in Religious Education (Cath. Inst. Paris). He has written books on Buddhism for non-Buddhists and on Christianity for non-Christians. He has also taught the subject of "World Religions" at university level. He has been awarded the "International Peace Prize" in 2010 by the American Bibliographical Institute for his efforts in promoting inter-religious and inter-racial harmony.

Salvation is not for one community but for all humanity.

"I appreciate your enlightening book on Religions. I don't know whether you are aware that I have always been interested in inter-religious thought and study.

I begin from the premise: If we believe that God created all human beings, we are all his children finding our different paths to him. In pre-Vatican Rome when our dogmatic theology professor kept on banging the desk and insisting "Extra ecclesiam nulla salus". (Latin for: "No salvation outside the Catholic Church.") I never agreed with him. Same today."

Archbishop Emeritus Nicholas Marcus Fernando, BA (London)
S.T.D. (Rome)

Foreword

by Rev. Dr. Marcus Braybrooke, Joint-President of the World Congress of Faiths and author of "Widening Vision: The World Congress of Faiths and the Growing Interfaith Movement" and other books.

At a time when religion is often hijacked by violent extremists or dismissed as irrelevant in the modern world, Dr. Antony Fernando's book *Understanding the Religions of Others (revised edition title is Building Bridges: Understanding the Religions of Others)* is a welcome and timely publication.

The first part gives a clear and amazingly concise summary of the development and teachings of Hinduism, Buddhism, Christianity and Islam. This makes the book very valuable for those who do not have time to consult lengthy religious encyclopedias. Dr. Fernando in his summaries dispels many of the prejudicial misunderstandings people have of religions other than their own and suggests that we all can learn from their central message.

He clarifies the role of the many gods and goddesses of popular Hinduism, making clear the essential Hindu belief that there is only one divine power: Brahman-Atman. He shows also that educated Hindus today seek to eradicate caste and poverty and have an openness to and respect for all religions. The Buddha's teaching on how to be free from suffering and to live in a permanent state of peace also has universal relevance at a time when so many people suffer from deep emotional disorders.

By including Judaism in the chapter on Christianity, Dr. Fernando makes clear the close links between the two religions. He points out that in the New English Bible, the first or Jewish part extends to 1164 pages, whereas the Christian New Testament has only 313 pages. He also says that the life-values upheld by Judaism "have the power to bring spiritual liberation to people of any race or nation" and were adopted by Christianity and Islam. He adds that "Jesus did nothing more than clarify to his listeners the notion of God-belief in the Jewish Bible". In his account of the life and teaching of Jesus, he emphasizes the message of God's care and forgiveness and the call to positive concern for others. He notes that in Jesus' parable of the sheep and the goats, people are judged by whether they have looked after those in need, and not by whether they are Hindu, Buddhist, Muslim or agnostic.

The chapter on Islam is also very sympathetic and dispels the negative image often created by the media. Because Islam continues to be "the spiritual anchor and guide to a major portion of humanity", it is important that members of other religions learn to appreciate the authentic teaching of the Prophet. Dr. Fernando points out the Prophet Muhammad's respect for other religions and his socio-political concern, although, as Dr. Fernando recognizes, the general trend of Islam to keep religion and state linked has both happy and unhappy sides.

The second part of the book looks at the meaning and relevance of religion today. In the past most people's religion was determined by their birth and so "inherited". They grew up to be members of the faith community to which their parents belonged and which the author calls "cultural religion". The word religion is also used for the meaning of life and the authentic way of living that an individual is "awakened to". The right way of living is illustrated in the life and teaching of the saints and seers of every religion. This is what the author refers to as "spiritual religion". Because of growing dissatisfaction with "inherited religion", believers who are aware of the riches of "awakened to" religion describe themselves as spiritual rather than as religious. The urgent need today if we are to build a united and a spiritually developed humanity, as Dr. Fernando rightly says in his concluding words, is to develop a "spiritual theology (or a spirituology) acceptable to all institutional religions and which focuses on the common root and the ultimate goal of all religions... If that happens, there is no doubt that the world we live in will soon be a place inhabited by people who, however racially and religiously distinct by birth will be uniformly aspiring for greater spiritual nobility."

This task should be a priority for religious leaders and teachers of every faith. In the words of Rabbi Tarfon: "It is not our responsibility to finish the work of perfecting the world, but we are not free to desist from it either".

Table of Contents

About Antony Fernando ii
Foreword iii
Introduction ix

    Value of Knowing Others' Religion ix

        Cultural Religion...ix
        Spiritual Religion x
        Knowledge of Religions xii

World Religions Part One: Hinduism 1

    Chapter 1 Origin and Fundamentals of Hinduism.................2

        1. The Main Belief 3
        2. Three Ways of Acquiring Awareness of Brahman 4
        3. The Four Stages of an Individual's Life (Ashrama) 5
        4. The Four Targets in Life 5

    Chapter 2 Sacred Texts of Hinduism 6

        Texts of the Shruti Category 6
        Texts of the Smriti Category 9

    Chapter 3 Hindu Gods and Goddesses 13

        1. God Shiva..13
        2. Natarajah..15
        3. Parvati 17
        4. Ganesh...18
        5. Skandha...19
        6. Vishnu 20
        7. Durga...21
        8. Kali...22
        Vehicles (Vahana)...23
        Religious Rites in the Temple 24
        Annual Festivals...25
        Understanding Hindu Forms of Worship.......................25

    Chapter 4 Hinduism of the Modern Era 28

        1. Raja Ram Mohan (1772- 1833) 29
        2. Dayananda Saraswathie Swami (1824-1883) 29
        3. Ramakrishna Paramahamsa (1834-1886) 30
        4. Vivekananda Swami (1862-1902) 30

    5. Mahatma Gandhi (1868-1848)...31

World Religions Part Two: Buddhism 33

  Chapter 1 A Religion With a Difference............................34
    Diverse Forms of Buddhism Today....................................35
    Value of Buddhism to Non-Buddhists...............................36

  Chapter 2 Life and Personality of the Buddha 38
    Home Life 38
    Renunciation 39
    Search...41
    Discovery Through Enlightenment..................................43
    Nirvāna as Liberation..44
    Preaching the Message..45
    The Super-humanity of the Buddha.................................46

  Chapter 3 The Sermon of the Four Noble Truths............48
    Text of Sermon 48
    Prelude and Conclusion 49
    Main Argument: Four Noble Truths 50
    First Noble Truth...50
    Second Noble Truth 51
    Third Noble Truth 51
    Fourth Noble Truth 52

  Chapter 4 The Eightfold Path 54
    Steps of the Eightfold Path 54
    1. Right View of Life (sammā ditthi).................................54
    2. Right Resolve (sammā sankappa) 55
    3. Right Speech (sammā vācā)..55
    4. Right Action (sammā kammantha) 55
    5. Right Livelihood (sammā ajiva) 55
    6. Right Effort (sammā vāyāma).......................................56
    7. Right Mindfulness (sammā sati) 56
    8. Right Insight-Meditation (sammā samādhi) 56
    Revolutionary Nature of the Eightfold Path 57

World Religions Part Three: Christianity (with Judaism)...61

  Chapter 1 Christianity Today and Christianity at the
  Beginning 62

1. Divisions in Contemporary Christianity 62
2. Forms of Church Today 63
3. Link of Christianity with Judaism 65

Chapter 2 Judaism the Mother-Religion of Christianity 68

1. Belief in One Life-giving God 70
2. Example of Abraham, Father of Monotheism 70
3. Living in Harmony with the Universe 72
4. Reason for Failure of Marriages 73
5. Basic Obligations of a Human Being 75

Chapter 3 The New Testament Miracle Stores in the Gospels 79

Gospels 79
Miracle-stories 80
Main Reason for Emphasis on Miraculous Healings 82
Jesus' Refusal to be a Wonder-worker 83
Miracles an Outcome of Faith 84

Chapter 4 Life and Teachings of Jesus 86

Life of Jesus 86
Meeting the Baptist 87
Ministry 88
Man of Prayer 88
End of the Ministry 90
What Jesus Taught 91

Chapter 5 Paul, The Formulator of Multi-Racial Christianity 97

Paul's Struggle with Christianity 98
What it is to be Christian According to Paul 107

World Religions Part Four: Islam 113

Chapter 1 Muhammad, the Founder of Islam 114

The Term "Islam" 114
Early Life 114
Marriage to Kadija 115
Life of Meditation 116
Conflicts at Start of Mission 117
Respect for Other Religions 118
Two Questions Posed, First About Monotheism 119

- Second Question: Islam's Religious Warfare 120
- Chapter 2 Koran the Sacred Text of the Muslims 122
  - Composition of the Koran 122
  - Main Beliefs of the Muslims 124
- Chapter 3 Religious Duties of Muslims, the Five Pillars of Islam 128
  - Profession of Faith (Sahada) 128
  - Daily Worship of God (Salat) 128
  - Almsgiving (Zakat) 132
  - The Month-long Fast of Ramadan (Sawm) 132
  - The Pilgrimage (Hajj) 133
  - The Formative Value of the Pillars 133
  - Islam Today 136

World Religions Part Five: Two Forms of Any Religion 137

- Chapter 1 Two Senses of Word "Religion" 138
  - Religion, Born-to 139
  - Religion, Awakened-to 140
  - View of Emile Durkheim 142
  - View of Rudolf Otto 143
- Chapter 2 Cultural Religion, Spiritual Religion 146
  - Cultural Religion – Inherited by Birth 146
  - Major Religions and Culture 147
  - Religion as Tradition 148
  - Spiritual Religion – A Way of Right Living 149
- Chapter 3 Two Ways of Practicing and Propagating Any Religion 151
  - Cultural Christian and Spiritual Christian 151
  - Purpose of the Book 152
  - A Matter for Theologians of All Religions 154

About iPubCloud.com 155

Introduction
Value of Knowing Others' Religion

This book which introduces a few important religions of today along with their similarities and dissimilarities may sound strange and even confusing to many readers. If it does, the cause is not so much the content of the book, but the readers for whom it is meant. Their unusualness is that while adhering to one religion (or even no religion) they show a deep interest in learning of the religions of others. My conviction is that there are today such individuals in each and every religion, and, however astounding it may sound, even among theologians of those religions. If open-minded believers keep an eye on other religions, it is for no other reason than to find out if those religions could help them understand more insightfully what is called "religion". There is no doubt that "religion" is a word used very widely in contemporary society. But whether it is used by anyone in the sense in which it is intended to be understood is seriously to be doubted. This is because, as we shall see more clearly in the last section of this book, the word "religion" has more than one sense to it, and of these, two are dominant: the cultural and the spiritual.

Cultural Religion

The first is what almost everybody takes as the ordinary sense of the word. The religion of that sense is what a person acquires through the process of birth and which we could simply call "inherited religion". Any child's religion is the religion of the mother, and that of the mother, the religion of the clan-community she belongs to. The human race, when taken as a whole, is nothing but a seemingly disorganized collection of such culturally united communities. The factor that is special about each such community is that their members claim to have one ancestral origin. They usually reside in one region. They have one mother-tongue. They practice one religion which they consider their own and which has been handed down without any change for ages from one generation to another. The functioning of the religion is maintained by a team of priests, monks or elders ordained for the purpose.

This type of religion has not only a religious authority but also a political authority. Often the religion of the king is the religion of the

Introduction

nation and if the king conquers another nation, that nation too then follows the religion of the conqueror.

The members of each such religion believe that, if they are faithful to the beliefs and rites upheld by the community, they will at the end of their corporeal life, be admitted to a heavenly abode reserved exclusively for them; and that those who fail to do so, will end up in an underworld or a hell where they will be tortured by devils and evil spirits. Those of clan-religions other than theirs too will undergo the same fate.

Those are the main elements of what most people take as their "Inherited Religion"; and since every inherited religion is an integral part of the culture of the given community, it can very simply be referred to as "cultural religion". The main task of any cultural religion is to keep the community united and its identity safeguarded.

Spiritual Religion

But this cultural version of religion is not sufficient for anybody to understand fully what religion really is. The main aim of religion when taken in its deeper spiritual form is not to separate clan communities from one another, but to make human beings aware of the deep mystery behind an individual's life and show them the way to personal salvation. Birth makes people racially and culturally different whereas death makes them humanly and spiritually identical. A Hindu, Buddhist or Christian and in the same way an Indian, Japanese or American ends his/her life exactly in the same way. Death is what establishes the fact that religious liberation or salvation is not restricted to one or another race but common to the entirety of mankind.

Religious liberation or salvation is not a reality that anybody can understand effortlessly. To understand what religions imply by the word "salvation", one has to look insightfully into one's own currant corporeal existence. There is no doubt that every individual seeks joy, peace, pleasure and fulfillment throughout one's life; but however unpalatable it may sound, it is equally true that the short span of anybody's life is filled with pain and suffering as also with fear and despair. The cultural community one belongs to, as also science and politics may have ways to bring about a certain amount of liberation from corporeal suffering but not to do away with it altogether. It is here that religion of the spiritual form intervenes to free people entirely from suffering.

The nature of salvation provided by spiritual religion is not apparent to the physical eye or the corporeal mind. It can be grasped only through insight, wisdom or the eye of faith. Further it becomes intelligible only to the person who can look in one glance at both the transient and the intransient parts of an individual's life. Of the two parts, the first is birth and the span of corporeal life that follows birth; the second is death and the incorporeal life that follows death.

If we take into consideration just the first part, the only fact that our physical senses can affirm is that a human being comes out of the womb of the mother. The natural conclusion which would flow from it is that the mother is the life-giver to the baby. But to be genuinely capable of giving life to any child, mustn't the life-giver have an awareness of at least how the heart of a child beats and how its blood circulates? Does a mother know anything about such facts vital for a life to operate?

Therefore, the simple conclusion that a person of any race or habitation has to come to is that the true life-giver cannot but be a Supreme Divine Power that has the ability to design, govern, protect and bring to its goal every form of entity inside or outside the universe. The form of that Power may not be definable or imaginable but it has been named by visionaries, sages, rishis, prophets and messiahs in the different sacred texts of the different religions through terms such as Brahman, Atman, Almighty God, Jehovah, Divine Spirit, or Allah. Any individual's life becomes operative only through the power of that invisible spirit.

The lesson taught by the second part of a human being's existence, or the one which starts with death, is equally eye-opening. Death is not a happening that any ordinary person joyfully looks forward to. In the way apparent to the corporeal senses, death is without any doubt, a total disappearance from earthly existence; and that idea of disappearance creates an apprehension in any living person. But for the insightful person there is nothing frightful in the reality of death. Death may be a cause for sorrow to the relatives who are left behind. But for the dying person it is a pleasant release and an entry to a happy life. All religions consider death as the doorway to final liberation or salvation.

Salvation, taken in its first and simplest sense, stands for permanent peace of mind, and that form of salvation can be achieved

Introduction

already in one's earthly span of existence. According to most visionaries, there are only two things to do to achieve salvation or peace of mind on earth. One is to keep constantly united in heart with the life-giving Divine Spirit, and the other is to treat with selfless care and concern all human beings irrespective of caste, color, creed or habitation.

But salvation, taken in its non-transient and permanent sense, starts, according to all religions, at the moment of an individual's corporeal death. At death everybody enters a life of eternal joy and peace which is a result of the individual's close unity with the Supreme Power of life. Seers and prophets in different religions have used different terms to express this state of ultimate liberation or salvation from suffering. The words most commonly used are Moksha, Nirvana, Heaven, Kingdom of God and Paradise.

One query that many people tend to ask at this point is whether the level of eternal peace and joy that all human beings acquire after death is the same for everybody. With our limited earthly human minds we may not be able to solve with precision questions such as these.

But when talking of levels of supra-earthly existence it is useful to take into account the notion of Rebirth or birth after death that Indian religions speak of along with Moksha and Nirvana, which are two Sanskrit words that imply salvation in its most perfect form. Rebirth can give the idea that, outside states parallel to Moksha and Nirvana, there are other levels of joy and peace. Such states provide an opportunity for further self-purification.

It is not impossible that Jesus could have meant something close to it, when according to the Gospel of John he said prior to his crucifixion, "There are many mansions in my father's house". Whatever may be the reality about levels of supernatural life, there is no need for anybody to doubt that life after death is always a state of unending peace and joy.

Knowledge of Religions

What has been said above rather sketchily about the two ways, in which the word "religion" could be understood, should make it clear to believers and non-believers alike that an unbiased examination of religions other than one's own could yield very enlightening insights to anybody into the mystery of life and religion.

Of these insights, three could be considered primary. First, they will see that both the cultural and spiritual forms of religion are indispensable to humanity as a whole. Second, they will see that, though religions of the cultural form are innumerable, religion of the spiritual form is, for all humanity, just one. Thirdly, they will see clearly which of the two forms is more conducive to their personal liberation. It is taking into consideration those aspects that, in this book, I have given more importance to spiritual religion than to cultural religion.

Antony Fernando, ThD, PhD

World Religions
Part One
Hinduism

Chapter 1
Origin and Fundamentals of Hinduism

Hinduism which is followed by over five hundred million people inhabiting the Indian peninsula is without any doubt one of the world's oldest religions. But it acquired the name "Hinduism" only in very recent times. The name was given by foreigners who came in contact with it. Both the words "India" and "Hinduism" derive from the name "Indus" by which the main river of the area is called.

Hinduism is not a religion that is easy to define or explain with clarity. It is not a religion that can be traced to one Founder. It hasn't an officially approved set of beliefs and rituals. It is worshipped in such a diversity of ways, that it is better referred to as an agglomeration of religions rather than one religion. But however diverse those forms of worship are, they are all like branches of a big tree that has one root. That root is the collection of sacred texts called the "Veda".

"Veda" which comes from the word "Vid" meaning "knowledge" is not a text that is commonly read or that many are closely acquainted with. But there is nobody who does not respect it. As a philosopher of the middle ages has declared anybody who does not reject it is a Hindu. Thus everybody in India who is not a Muslim, Buddhist, Christian or Sikh is a Hindu. Hinduism can be found outside India in countries to which Hindus have migrated. Bangladesh, Malaysia and Sri Lanka are such countries. In the West too, there is today a large number of non-Indians who follow Hinduism.

India is a country in which people have lived from very ancient times. Its inhabitants have belonged to diverse clans and tribes. Even 2500 years before the Christian era, tribes had lived in it. The more prominent among them are those with a brownish skin and curly hair called the Dravidians. When they formed the major section of the population, that is, in the era between 1200 and 1500 BC, a group entered the land from the North West. They were referred to as "Ariya" or "Ariyan", a word meaning "noble".

Since they had acquired the art of horsemanship and were acquainted with equestrian battle methods, it was not difficult for them to gain control of the Dravidians and other tribal groups that inhabited the country. The Ariyans spoke an Indo-European language.

The Sanskrit language is an outcome of it. Their religion and culture contained elements belonging to those of the Greeks, Romans and Iranians.

Unfortunately still today we know little of the civilization of the Pre-Aryian Dravidian era. According to the findings of scholars so far, Pre-Aryian culture had been of a very high standard. They have had an urban culture of a very high level. Of the languages spoken by the Dravidians four have had a very highly developed literature. Tamil is one of them. Tamil literature goes back to over 2000 years.

Due to the limited nature of the knowledge we possess of Dravidian culture, it is difficult for us to say if it would have had any direct influence on Hinduism. What we can safely say at the present moment is that Hinduism owes its origin to the Ariyan civilization.

Even though Hinduism is treated as a religion rooted in God-belief, the entity called "god" is explained by its followers in different ways. Some affirm that God is one divine being. That divine being, for some, is a personal reality and for others, an impersonal one. Some adhere to the belief in a large number of gods and goddesses. But these gods and goddesses are considered representatives of the one and same invisible God. The diversity in the explanations given to the Hindu concept of God goes down to the books of the Veda tradition. In the way underlined in the "Rig Veda", "Truth is one, but teachers call it by different names".

It is not easy to indicate what Hindus consider as the fundamentals of their religion. Those considered the most vital can be summed up under the four following headings:

1. The Main Belief

The truth that is considered the most fundamental is the one referred to as "Brahman" (not to be confused with "Brahmin" a member of the priestly caste). Brahman is the all-pervading divinity and the soul of the universe. Brahman can be personal or impersonal. It can be presented in diverse symbolic forms. The only eternal and ever unchanging reality is Brahman. All sensually perceptible objects are impermanent and temporary. Those who see them as permanent are under an illusion (Maya).

2. Three Ways of Acquiring Awareness of Brahman

There are several ways to acquire knowledge of that reality called "Brahman". Three are primary. The first is the path of insightful meditation or the "Jnana Marga". Since Brahman is the soul (Atman) of the universe, realizing through meditation that God and one's own self are identical is that first way. The second is "Bhakti Marga" or the path of devotion. A follower of that way selects one god or goddess from the Hindu pantheon and keeps united with that deity through forms of worship cherished by the deity.

The third is the path of duty-fulfillment, the "Karma Marga". In Indian society all human beings are born endowed with a special task to fulfill throughout their life. A member of the priestly caste has to offer sacrifice in the temple. A member of the soldier caste has to fight for the protection of the country. A member of the farmer caste has to cultivate food and look after cattle that give milk. A member of the serf caste has to engage in activities such as washing and cleaning. Each person fulfilling his or her duty is united with the Supreme Divinity.

The three ways to spirituality mentioned above show how insightful Hindu Rishis have been when speaking of the supreme divine reality that human beings have to be in communication with to achieve spiritual perfection. All the religions we know of, whether polytheistic or monotheistic look at god (or gods) as a personal entity. Since what is called "a person" is the highest form of entity that human beings are aware of, it is justifiable that the concept of person be utilized to make the invisible divine reality imaginable. In monotheistic religions such as Judaism, Christianity and Islam, God is looked at as one person. But we must not forget that thinking of god as one person is only a picturization of an imperceptible uncountable reality.

Realizing that fact, Hindu seers have tried to surpass picturization. Of the three ways only the second the Bhakti-marga leaves room for picturization. Simple Hindu folk may worship different gods and goddesses taking them as male and female persons. Theirs is what we could call "personified polytheism". In the first, or the Jnana-marga the supreme divine reality is considered too transcendental to be personalized and so, what they follow is a form of "non-personified theism". That impersonal reality is to be reached through meditation and experienced through mystical union.

In the third or the Karma marga, the concept is again impersonal and even just experiential. God is not an object to be worshipped on altars. Access to God is by the right fulfillment of one's day to day social obligations. That way of worship may be called "non-personified experiential theism".

The Hindu approach to the divine reality is more subtle than that of monotheistic religions. But it is not impossible that, by its effort to prevent people from imagining God as a person, Hinduism has something more to offer to people trying to comprehend the divine side of life.[1]

3. The Four Stages of an Individual's Life (Ashrama)

A person who accepts Brahman as the supreme reality, particularly a member of the Brahmin or priestly class, has to organize his life in four stages called "Ashrama". The first stage is called that of the "Brahmachari". At that stage one should be a student of the "Veda" and spend a celibate life. The second is that of the "Grihastha" or the householder. At that stage he is married and his main task is to bring up children.

The third namely the "Vanaprastha" or hermit, and the fourth the "Sannyasi" or ascetic are two stages one could freely choose from. But today neither of them is considered obligatory.

4. The Four Targets in Life

There are four targets in life that a Hindu is expected to strive for. The first is economic security (Artha). Nobody can live a wholesome life without material necessities such as food and shelter. The second is sexual fulfillment (Kama). Love and marriage are indispensable for achieving fulfillment in anyone's life. The third is conformity to right religious values (Dharma) or the fulfillment of laws given by God. The fourth is the achievement of self-liberation (Moksha). This is a sublime state of mind which demands withdrawal from earthly desires and the practice of contentment with whatever one receives. It can be asserted that, as a general rule, every Hindu accepts those elements as requirements for a life as a genuine Hindu.

---

[1] Rig Veda 1: 25

Chapter 2
Sacred Texts of Hinduism

The sacred writings of the Hindus are divided into two categories. One is called "Shruti" which means "heard" or "listened to". Those books are believed to contain truths that sages have discovered by listening to universal nature and their own enlightened conscience. Those books are treated as revelations by God.

The second is called "Smriti" a word meaning "memory" or "retained by memory". Though they too are considered important sacred texts, they are not treated as revealed by God. But a book of that second category called the "Bhagavad Gita" and a few others similar to it are considered by the Hindu masses as equal in rank to those of the first category and are treated as texts revealed by God.

5. Texts of the Shruti Category

Three types of books belong to the Shruti category. Those of the first type and considered the most important, are called the "Vedas". Those of the second which are treated as commentaries of the "Vedas" are the "Brahmanas". Those of the third are the "Upanishads". Since the Upanishads are the last books to be produced on Veda thought, they are referred to also as "Vedanta" (Veda-anta) the end or the conclusion of the Vedas.

1. Veda Texts

There are four volumes that belong to the category of Veda texts. They are the Rig Veda, the Yajur Veda, the Sama Veda and the Atharva Veda, Since "Veda" means knowledge, the Vedic texts can be treated as books of "knowledge" or of "knowledge endowed by God".

Since the word "Rig" attached to the first means "praise" the Rig Veda is treated as the book dedicated to praise of God. It is considered the oldest of the Veda books. For centuries it was preserved through group memory and committed to writing only between 1800 and 1500 BC. The main gods subjected to praise in it are Agni, Indra and Varuna. One hymn sung in praise of god Varuna may be translated as follows:

He knows the path of birds that fly across the sky.

He is the lord of the seas and so he recognizes the ships that sail on them.

The wind blows wide. It goes up. It is powerful. He knows the paths of the wind.

He knows the gods who reside above, but still in accordance with divine design he resides among ordinary people and sits down beside them.

Even though sitting with ordinary folk, being supreme in wisdom he controls everything.

Oh god Varuna, listen to my plea. On this passing day be compassionate to me.

I ask for your help.

Endowed with supreme wisdom, you are the lord of all.

You are the king of this world and the world above.

Listen to us and give us joy and relief from pain.[1]

The songs we come across in the Yajur Veda are practically the same as those of the Rig Veda except for the fact that for the benefit of priests who use them in ritual services, some explanations have been added to them in simplified prose. Of the Veda series of books the last to be composed is the Atharva Veda. It gets its name from the priest Atharva who composed it.

2. Brahmana Texts

The Brahmanas, listed second, are a series of ritual books meant for Brahmin priests who use the Veda hymns in the ritual services. They are supposed to have been composed between 800 and 500 BC. They are full of legends and myths which are a requirement for making ordinary folk understand and appreciate rituals.

3. Upanishads or Vedanta Texts

The third group of books of the "Shruti" category is the Upanishads. The term "Upanishad" (Upa-ni-shad) is a combination of the words meaning "seated nearby". This is because their content was taught by sages to students seated by their side. The teachings of the Upanishads are considered to be at the bottom of the entire religious and philosophical thought of Indian society.

---

[1] Please note: The long sounding vowels of Sanskrit terms are underlined in the English words, v.g. Jnana Marga.

The Upanishads are said to consist of 108 volumes. Of these what are considered to be the oldest and so given primacy are the two called Aranyaka Upanishad and the Chandogya Upanishad. Of the doctrines dealt with in the Upanishads the one that could be considered the most enlightening is that on the identity of Brahman and Atman.

Beyond doubt, this universe was originally Brahman. Everyone in it felt "I am Brahman". Anything that existed in it was He. If any god grasped the truth about Brahman he became Brahman. Philosophers as also all human beings were the same. Anybody who subscribed to the Brahman reality saying "I am Brahman" became the only true existing reality.[2]

Truly the whole universe is Brahman. Everybody should worship it realizing that he came out of it, that he breathes within it and that one day he will be absorbed into it.

The soul within my heart is very small. It is smaller than a grain of paddy or a mustard seed. It is smaller than the seed of a grass-shoot or even the kernel of that seed. On the other side, the soul in my heart is bigger than the earth, bigger than the totality of space, bigger than the sky. It is bigger than every one of the worlds.

What provides the foundation to any action, to any work, to any aspiration, to any smell, to any taste, to the entire universe is the great soul Atman which functions silently and without motion from within my heart. It is Brahman. When I leave here I will see myself dwelling within it.[3]

A second doctrine that is lengthily dealt with in the Upanishads is that of Karma (Law of reward and punishment for good and bad actions) and Rebirth.

Those who lead a noble life on earth will be reborn after death in a noble form and enjoy a painless life. They will be born as members of the priestly (brahmin) caste, the administrative (kshatriya) caste or the businessmen (vaishya) caste. But those who lead bad lives on earth will be reborn as a being living an unhappy and painful life. They will be reborn as a dog, a pig or a human being of the lowest caste.[4]

---

[2] Brihad Aranyaka Up 1:4
[3] Chandogya Up 3:14
[4] Chandogya Up 5:10

6. Texts of the Smriti Category

Though the books of the Smriti category hold a secondary place in comparison with the Shruti texts, they are the ones that make the message of the Vedas accessible to the ordinary folk. Five types of books belong to it. The first is called the Dharmashastra (and at times by the specific name of Smriti) are codes of Law. They show how religion is to be structured as a society or institution. The second is called Itihasa (literally "history"). They are epic poems that illustrate the teachings of right religion by portraying the achievements and adventures of India's national heroes. The third which is termed Purana (literally "old" or "ancient") describe the history of the race. The fourth called Agama (literally "religion") describe the popular forms of worship. The last called Dharshana contain the teachings of sages on right living.

1. Dharmashastra Texts

The Dharmashastra contains books of law used in the government of the country. They appeared in different versions in diverse stages of Indian history. The code of Manu called "Manu Samhita" or "Manu Smriti" is the one considered the earliest among them. Two extracts from it are as follows:

Learn the divine law practiced by those educated in the Veda. Those who overcome hatred and wrong forms of love adhere to that law in their hearts. Those who ignore the law and work exclusively for their personal gain engage in a fruitless search of happiness.[5]

To the extent possible, everybody should fulfill with a joyful heart, the duty of generosity. If a respectable person is in need, that person's need should be answered without any reduction of the respect due to him. If a poor person is in need of help, he should be helped. If due to lack of resources, the full help cannot be given, at least the part possible should be given ungrudgingly.

Anybody who receives even a pittance of help when in need, may become the donor's savior someday. The giver of drink is rewarded with joy in his heart. Giver of food enjoys a lasting inner pleasure.[6]

---

[5] Manu 2:1
[6] Manu 4: 227-229

2. Itihasa Texts

The two epic poems of Mahabharatha and Ramayana which narrate the heroic deeds of India's national heroes belong to the Itihasa category. The purpose of those books is to explain the religious philosophy of the Vedas in as striking a manner as possible to the ordinary people.

The essence of the Mahabharatha is summed up in the poem called the "Bhagavad Gita", "the Song of the Lord". It is considered the story that depicts best the inner thinking pattern of the Indian people. The poem is constructed as a conversation between a soldier called Arjuna and the lord Krishna who is disguised as the rider of a chariot. The conversation starts when Arjuna enters the battle field and realizes that the foe he is expected to fight with is composed of his own kith and kin. The situation makes him doubt whether in the circumstances he should go into battle or not. In a confused mind he decides not to fight and leaves the battle field. If he left the battle field, there would be no war and no lives will be lost. But then the hard hearted and evil minded king Duryodana will overcome his army and do harm to his people.

It is at this moment that the lord Krishna intervenes. Explaining to him his duty as a soldier, he dispels Arjuna's state of doubt. The lesson that he teaches Arjuna is this. Every human being must fulfill the duty entrusted to him at his birth. It is not his concern to judge the outcome of his activity. Arjuna is a soldier by the profession he has inherited. He should fulfill that duty. But he should execute that task without hatred or selfishness and in full accordance with religious principles.

As a member of the kshatriya (soldier) caste, your duty is to fight in the battle field. You have nothing better to do than to engage in war in keeping with religious principles. Thus there is no reason for you to be in doubt as to whether you should fight or not. You are fortunate that the opportunities for battle have been endowed to you, as it were automatically, without your having to go in search of them on your own. The doors of the higher worlds are open to you. But if, for one reason or another you abstain from going into this battle, you will fall into the sin of infidelity to duty. You will thereby lose the prestige due to a duty-fulfilling fighter.

From then onwards the lord Krishna goes to explain the dignity that a human being can achieve through fidelity to duty. One lesson he teaches is as follows:

Any human being must strive to uplift himself to the highest level of life and not degrade himself to the lowest level. The tool for either is the same. It is the mind. The friend as also the foe of the Great Soul (Atman) imprisoned in the body is the mind. For the person who keeps his desires under control, the mind is the best friend. For the person who cannot keep his mind under control, the mind is the worst foe.

The person whose mind is under control has entered into the Universal Soul (Atman). He has achieved peace of mind. For such a person, joy and sorrow, heat and cold, honor and dishonor are the same. The person who has uplifted his human behavior up to the highest level is a yogi (one united with God). He has a right grasp of life. His life is of a super-natural or spiritual level. He has full control of himself. He sees everything whether stone or gold in the same way.

A supernatural being must always concentrate on the Great Soul (Atman). He should be capable of living alone without a distracted mind. He should carefully control his mind. He should keep it free of wrong desires and attachments.[7]

The other great book of the Itihasa category is the Ramayana. It contains an account of another national hero namely Rama, a royal prince. He had to leave the palace because of a plot devised by a second queen of her father and her son. He lived in exile in a forest for 14 years.

In the meantime, Rama's faithful wife Seetha is kidnapped by a cruel devil. When Rama failed in all his efforts to find his wife, he gets the assistance of a divinely powered monkey called Hanuman. The powerful monkey succeeds to bring Rama and Seetha together. Today Rama, Seetha and Hanuman are respected by a large number of Hindus and are even worshipped as gods.

3. *Purana Texts*

Purana are books which contain stories of gods and goddesses. Those stories were created in very early times. Stories of god Brahma are sacred to Brahma worshippers; those of god Vishnu to the

---

[7] Bhagavad Gita 2.31-338

Vaisnavites and those of god Shiva to the Shaivites. Those stories have contributed much to the education of the Indian people.

4. *Agama* Texts

Books called Agama (literally "religion") contain descriptions of various gods and the way they are to be worshipped. The ways of worshipping god Vishnu, god Shiva and goddess Shakti are dealt with in separate texts.

The treatise on God Vishnu is called "Pancha-rathra" and is sacred to the Vaishnavites. That on Shiva is called "Shaiva-Siddhanta" and is sacred to the Shaivaites. The books that treat of goddess Shakti as the primary truth are called "Tantra". Goddess Shakthi is sometimes called the Universal Mother.

5. *Dharshana* Texts

Books of Dharshana (literally "philosophy") consist of expositions of a number of philosophy systems. The books are not meant for ordinary folk but for scholars and intellectuals. Six systems are expounded in them. Taking the inter-connection between some of them they are generally coupled together and divided into three different groups. (1) Nyaya philosophy of Gautama and the Vaisheshika philosophy of Kanada, (2) Sankya philosophy of Kapila and the Yoga philosophy of Pathanjali, (3) Mimansa philosophy of Jaimini and the Vedantha philosophy of Badarayana.

All these texts which belong to the Smriti category are treated as works deriving from the Veda roots. The ultimate aim of the texts of Dharmashastra, Itihasa, Purana, Agama and Dharshana is assumed to be the same as of all the texts of the Shruti category, the Vedas, the Brahmanas and the Upanishads. That aim is to redeem human beings of their inner voices, and help them to be united with the ultimate divine reality, and thus become perfect human beings. For the achievement of that aim both the Shruti and Smriti texts strive to create the right environment in society and in the hearts of individuals.

Chapter 3
Hindu Gods and Goddesses

If we take Hinduism according to its philosophy, there is not the least doubt that there is only one divine power. It is called "Brahman-Atman". In its transcendental or celestial form, God is Brahman. In its immanent or within-universe form it is Atman.

But Hindu philosophy and popular Hindu beliefs are not identical. The Hindu masses venerate a large number of gods and goddesses. These gods and goddesses and also their names and attributes have changed from time to time. Today they are different even from region to region.

If we take all the patterns in which gods and goddess are worshipped, we can divide Hindu believers into three different groups. One is the group called Shaivites. Their main object of veneration is god Shiva. The second, and the more numerous, group, are the Vaishnavites. They take Vishnu as their supreme god. The third group venerates goddess Shakti and is called Shaktas. The word "shakti" means "power" or "energy". In a way very particular to Indian thought, the Shaktas personalize that divine power and conceive it as residing in the consort or wife of Shiva, Vishnu or any other god. The female counterpart of any god is called "Shakti".

But according to Dharmashastra texts, a third god called Brahma (not to be confused with Brahaman) is also worshipped by the Hindus. The Three gods Brahma, Vishnu and Shiva are considered the Triad or the Trinity of Hindus. But unlike in the past, temples dedicated to Brahma are very few in India today.

7. 1. God Shiva

The branch of Hindu devotees called Shaivites, venerate Shiva as their supreme deity. They attribute to him all the powers and characteristics that devotees of Brahma and Vishnu attribute to their deities.

In the view of Shaivites, of everything existing in the world, god Shiva is the creator, protector and destroyer. The idea that Shiva or any other god is both the creator and the destroyer of life, or in other words, the master of both life and death could appear illogical to some. But nobody can deny that physical life and death on one side and supra-physical after-death life on the other are integral elements of the reality of life. It is probably with the aim of finding the right solution to the mystery of life at both the physical and spiritual levels that Hindus have combined all those aspects in the pictures they have drawn of their gods and goddesses.

God Shiva is called by a number of names. The more common among them are: Rudra, Sadha̱sivam, Aran, I̱shvaran, Maheshwaran, Nadesan, Natarajah, Sangaran, Mukkannan, Seetambaran, Parameshwaran.

If god Shiva is called by such a large number of names it is because, in the view of scholars, he is the representative of a large number of gods and goddesses in different periods and different regions acknowledged by different groups of Indians. Temples dedicated to gods and goddesses bearing such names are found almost in every region inhabited by Hindus.

God Shiva is not just the eternal power behind all existing things and their evolution. He is also the emblem of the divineness that a human being is expected to achieve.

Some features of an image of god Shiva are as follows: He is seated on a bull (nandi) his vehicle. In one of his hands is a trident or a three pronged fork. The trident is for self-defense and for attacking enemies. It is also a symbol of the invincible power he wields over the universe.

In his other hand is a drum. It shows that he is the one who provides the rhythm for the spiritual journey that a human being has to engage in. There is a third eye on his forehead. It is through that eye he diffuses life, light and heat throughout the universe.

Around his neck is a cobra, a snake which emits poison when it stings. But god Shiva is immune to poison. The cobra is a symbol of Shiva's immortality.

The river Ganges flows out of the top loft of his hair. People go to a river in search of purity. God Shiva is the symbol of purity. Around his neck is a chain of human skulls. It is a reminder to everybody that though humanity gets wiped out from generation to generation, divine power is everlasting.

Shaivites present their god Shiva in diverse forms and symbols. The most popular among them is what is called the "Shiva-lingam", a short pillar of about two feet made of mud, stone or marble. In the way the Shiva-lingam is explained by some, "Shiva" stands for "complete fortune" and "lingam" for "symbol", in which case "Shiva-lingam" is a reference to the ultimate fortune of humanity and of the universe.

Shiva

According to some others however, since the word "lingam" is used for the male as also female sexual organ, Shiva lingam is a reference to Shiva as the super power that gives life to everything in the universe. This phallic symbol could have been absorbed by the Hindus from earlier tribal cults. Another explanation is that since it is, as it were, formless because it does not copy any living being, it is well suited to represent a divine being which cannot be put into the forms of any existing being that we know of.

8. 2. Natarajah

God Shiva is considered the authority and the creator of the art of dance. For that reason he is also called Natarajah (nata= dance; rajah=king). Every one of the 108 styles of the Indian art of dancing is said to have originated from him.

Hindu Gods and Goddesses

Natarajah

The dance of Shiva as shown in the popular Natarajah images is considered an exhibition of the three ways in which the universe is created, safe-guarded and destroyed. It is during the festival called the "Maha Shiva Ratri" (the night of Great Shiva) that he is said to have kept his fighting tool, the trident aside, and performed the dance.

As he dances, he steps on a dwarfed human being crushing him with his drum.

The dwarfed being represents the lower or the earthly self that a human being has to crush to acquire selflessness. The dancing individual represents the inner self liberated from selfishness and united with the divine soul, Atman.

In one of his four hands is a circular instrument which indicates the rhythm for the dance. In his second hand is a flame of fire which gives anybody the light required to see the path of right living.

The other two hands display two gestures. The one pointing upwards is one of granting blessings. The other pointing downwards is one of taking the earth as witness to his stability and strength.

The spread-out hair forms a halo behind the face. This shows the stability of a liberated individual. When all the aspects of the Natarajah dance are taken together we can say that it conveys a valuable as also a joyful spiritual message to the viewer.

9. 3. Parvati

Just as diverse names are used to indicate Lord Shiva, diverse names are used also for his wife and children. The word commonly used for the wife of any god is "Shakti" (literally "energy" or "power"). The first name used for the shakti of Lord Shiva is "Parvati". Other names used are, Minachi, Uma, Parashakthi, Gowri, and Ambikai.

Though Shiva is declared the creator, protector and the destroyer of the universe, it should be noted that he gets his power for all that from his female partner Parvati. In Hindu thought the power of a god resides always in his female partner. Just like the lord Shiva himself, his consort Parvati is looked at, from one side as a very kind-hearted, benign person and from another as a harmful cruel and destructive personality.

Parvati

This is because according to Indian philosophy, the arising of life cannot be separated from its vanishing. In the daily schedule of the universe, morning ceases when noon comes and noon ceases when night comes. It is the same with everything in the universe. Life in it comes and goes. Even though Parvati, the shakti of Lord Shiva, is the one to whom most prominence is given, we must not forget that the shaktis of gods Brahma and Vishnu are also deeply venerated.

The shakti of god Brahma is "Saraswathi" (literally, "flowing regularly"). She is like a river that flows and gives fertility to the surrounding earth. When taken in the sense of flowing thought, Saraswathi is regarded as the patron of all academic sciences and arts. Giving enlightenment to human beings is her main task.

The female consort of god Vishnu is "Laxmi". She is considered the sponsor of beauty and of material fortune. For that reason among ordinary Hindus she takes even a more beloved position than even Saraswathi.

10. 4. Ganesh

Of the sons of Shiva the one considered as the first is Ganesh. His name, composed of the two words "gana" and "isha", means "head of the minor or inferior deities". He is also called by other names such as Ganapathi, Gajanana, Vinayakar, and Vigneshvaran. Very simply he is also called "Pillaiyar" which means "son". He is considered an unmarried individual.

Ganesh is supposed to be the god who helps people to overcome obstacles. There is a general belief that without the assistance of god Ganesh, no obstacle can be overcome.

God Ganesh is generally depicted as a human being with an elephant face. One of the tusks of the head is broken. His stomach is heavily bloated up. He is seated keeping one leg on the other.

Ganesh

There is a rat on the ground at his feet with some edibles in its hands. It seems to be awaiting the god's permission to eat it. The rat is generally explained as a symbol of the human being in search of genuine sublimity. The rat is also considered the companion and the vehicle of god Ganesh.

The two big ears portray two qualities required for acquisition of knowledge. They are attentive listening and reflective judgment.

The extensive ears and the large head indicate that in a previous existence of his, god Ganesh had listened to the inner reality of life and subjected what he heard to objective judgment.

The gesture of keeping only one foot on the ground is an indication that he is a person with determination. He had developed to the highest level his intelligence and power of understanding. He is free of cupidity and hatred

His outsized but well-filled stomach shows that he has no hunger whatsoever. His stomach is filled not with earthly food but with the food that elevates a human being to divine life. According to a popular legend, at a festival he attended no type of food served there could satisfy him. His hunger was appeased only by a handful of fried rice given him by his father god Shiva.

There is a lotus flower in his hand. According to the commonly accepted Indian tradition, the lotus is a symbol of the fullness of spiritual life that a human being should achieve.

11. 5. Skandha

The second son of god Shiva is Skandha. He is considered the god of war and holds the rank of a general in the divine army. When taken in that capacity, he is shown as a person having six faces and twelve hands. For that reason he is also called Shanmugam (shan=six; mughan=faces). The faces enable him to see all around. The large number of hands enables him to grip as many weapons as possible. His main war tool is a sharply pointed heavy pole.

Though described as a god of war, most devotees treat god Skandha as a very kind-hearted and com- passionate deity. He too is called by a number of names, such as Kandasamy, Kathi-resa (Karthi-keya) Aru-mugham, Kumara-samy, Murukhan, Katharagama, and Subramanium.

God Skandha is treated as a god of war only in its spiritual application. He fights only against the mind-blinding tendencies such as greed and hatred.

Skandha

What is taken as the companion or vehicle of god Skandha is the peacock. There is a popular view that because of its beauty, the peacock is a self-exhibiting proud animal. Man too similarly is a victim of the vice of pride. To achieve inner sublimity, man must give up thinking too much of himself and overcome his pride. He should strive to acquire selflessness.

In the images of god Skandha, there is a snake along with the peacock. The snake too is taken as a symbol of self-centeredness. According to a legend accepted by some Hindus, god Skandha is married and has two wives. One is "Devayani", and the other, from the tribe of the primitive veddhas, is "Valli". According to scholars god Skandha may not be just an imaginatively devised figure. He could well have been a real king of a given era who had shown great prowess in battle.

12. 6. Vishnu

As alluded to earlier, Shiva is considered the supreme deity only in certain regions such as Sri Lanka. But in most places and India itself, predominance is given to god Vishnu.

Vishnu

Vishnu appears in only a few hymns of the Rig Veda. But in the Mahabharatha he is the supreme deity alongside Shiva. Vishnu is called by other names such as Krishna, Narayan, Hari, Kannan, Kovinnan and Perumal.

The devotees of Vishnu are called Vaishna-vites or Shri Vashnavas. For those believers, Vishnu is the greatest god, and the sole deity of whom other gods are but aspects.

God Vishnu is respected in Buddhism too. He is worshipped as a god by Sinhala Buddhists in Sri Lanka. Among Hindus, the Buddha is considered an apparition or "avatar" of God Vishnu.

13. 7. Durga

Goddess Parvati is represented in two other forms too and under two other names. One is Durga and the other Kali. The shape given to both is somewhat fearsome to look at.

The word Durga means "inaccessible" or "difficult to approach". Since she is taken as the personification of the creative, protective and destructive power of all the gods, she becomes unapproachable and even un-understandable. But since she is considered also the mother of the universe she is also treated as the symbol of kind-heartedness and compassion.

Durga

In statues and pictures she is shown as a woman riding a lion and carrying a number of war tools in her many hands. What the picture symbolically says is that she is the person who fights against evil. She fights evil only to protect and propagate the good. Devotees seek her help mainly to overcome bad thoughts and desires which dominate them. They feel that Durga's assistance is indispensable for them to achieve liberation (moksha).

14. 8. Kali

The second version of goddess Parvati, namely that of "Kali", is even more fearful to look at. She is without clothes. Her body is covered with a piece of cloth which hangs from her neck like an apron. A number of hands cut from human bodies hang from the apron. Around her neck is a chain made of skulls. At her feet is a head cut off with the sword she holds in her hand. What she stands on is a human corpse. That corpse is said to be that of her husband, god Shiva.

The word Kali comes from the word "kala" meaning "time". Time cannot be seen. It cannot be touched. The only way to visualize it is through the form of goddess Kali.

It is she who brings life as also death. The builder of the universe as also its destroyer is Kali. Kali has the power over both the sides of reality. However unpleasant it may be, nobody can ignore the death or the destroyer side of life. Cemeteries and battle fields keep him reminded of it.

Kali

But what opens the door to life, liberation and eternal life, is also Time. Liberation is possible only for the one who surpasses the limitations of Time. What Kali portrays is not so much the destructive side of divine power but the painful side of Time. She also shows the way to go beyond Time. She is also the picture of the eternal night of true peace and joy.

It is she that puts even god Shiva into the realm that gives him power to create the universe. Not from just one side, but from all sides she is the power of all the gods combined.

15. Vehicles (Vahana)

A description of the Hindu gods and goddesses is not complete without a word on what are called their "vehicles" or "vahana". All gods and goddesses are believed to travel on (or at least be accompanied by) animals specially designated to them. The vehicle of god Brahma is the goose, or swan (hansa). That of Vishnu is the eagle (garuda). Shiva's vehicle is the bull (nandi). Indra's, is the elephant. The vehicle of Ganesh is the rat and of Durga, the lion. The lesson conveyed by animal vehicles is a simple one. It shows that human beings must overcome the animal aspects of their behavior to go beyond the earthly to the supra-earthly.

16. Religious Rites in the Temple

Even though there is a place for religious worship in every home, even in that of the poorest, the temple is the place to which they go together for services conducted by priests. Before we say anything about religious rites held in temples, we must have a clear grasp of the strange way adopted by Hindu people to look at the place or temple in which religious services are held. They look at the temple from an angle very different from that of devotees of other religions.

For the Hindus, the temple is not just a place of worship and prayer. It is the place where their favorite god or goddess resides. Recognizing that, they remove their footwear as they enter the temple. They know that they are now treading on sacred ground. As they enter the building they sound a bell hung above the door, as it were, to inform the deity that they are entering his or her house. As they approach the altar on which the deity is enthroned, they place their joined palms on their heads and prostrate themselves making their knees, elbows and forehead touch the ground.

After venerating the deity they offer a gift at its altar. The gift does not have to be an article of economic value. God Krishna has made this clear in the Bhagavadgita. "I accept with love whatever is offered to me in genuine piety. What is offered could be just a leaf, a flower, a fruit or a drop of water".

The image of the main god is enthroned at the altar on the opposite side of the entrance. There are shrines to other gods on the other sides. The altar of the main god is considered the holy of holies and only an ordained priest can go close to it. Treating the image as a living being, the priest's task is to bathe it wash it and adorn it with new clothes. After that he offers to the image flowers, incense, food and lights.

The offering of lights which is the last item is considered the most sacred moment. Offering of lights is done by waving a lit candelabra round the head of the deity. At this moment a conch shell is used to make a trumpet sound. The assembly joins the trumpet sound shouting "haro, hara" (an equivalent of "Glory to God, glory to God"). The offering or "puja" ends with the distribution by the priest of a morsel of blessed food to the participants. The blessed food called "Prasad" is as a rule composed of cooked milk rice.

17. Annual Festivals

Like members of all religions the Hindus too celebrate annual festivals. Of these, the two most important are "Maha Shiva Ratri" and "Deepavali". Maha Shiva Ratri, special particularly to the section of Hindus called the Shaivties, is a fasting festival. Its special importance is that it is on this day that they prepare the ash for applying on their foreheads. The ash is made from cow-dung rolled into balls and dried in the sun. On the night of the Maha Shiva Ratri, they are heaped on coconut husks or chaff of wheat and made to burn throughout the night. The following morning the ash is collected into containers and preserved for use till the next festival.

"Deepavali" or "Deevali" (literally a string of lights) is a festival of lights coming down from ancient times. Its main feature is that on that night all buildings, lands, trees, streets are elaborately decorated with lamps. According to the Bhagavata Purana, the festival commemorates the domination of an evil demon-king who harmed human beings as also minor gods. Those who suffered from him invoked god Vishnu and asked him to destroy the demon king, but since this demon-king had engaged in some ascetical exercises in his youth, Vishnu was reluctant to punish him at once.

But when he saw that there was no end to his misdeeds, he engaged god Krishna, (actually another apparition or version of god Vishnu himself) to catch him and kill him. When this demon king saw lord Krishna he understood his sinful behavior and not only regretted his crimes but thanked the lord Krishna for bringing him liberation. What the story teaches is that evil in the world can be destroyed not by killing evil-doers, but by changing their hearts and redeeming them of their evil behavior.

18. Understanding Hindu Forms of Worship

The description of the Hindu gods and goddesses and the Hindu forms of worship given above will no doubt appear incomprehensible to anyone unacquainted with Indian thought patterns. As a help to such individuals, all that we can do is add a few observations to be taken for what they are worth. We restrict ourselves to just three.

(1) The first is that Hinduism is not a religion that enforces on its followers a fixed set of beliefs and rituals. Unlike in other religious institutions, Hinduism has no central teaching authority to control its

forms of worship. Anybody can follow the tradition of one's region or tribal group. Thus individuals are left free to follow their own insights in the practice of religion creating thereby also their own variations of gods and goddesses.

Gods and goddesses in Hinduism should not be mistaken for actual supra-terrestrial entities. Pictures shown of them are so incongruous that they cannot represent real beings. The deities combine features that are usually not combinable. The nose of one god is an elephant's trunk. Another has several hands and heads. One god wears a cobra round the neck and rides in the air on the back of a bull. One goddess wears an apron on which hands cut out of human bodies are made to hang.

Such illustrations of deities displayed in temples and shrines cannot therefore be portraits of existing entities; but they cannot be ignored and set aside because they are valuable mental creations which illustrate the complex mystery of human life.

Earthly existence too is a strange combination of seemingly uncombinable facets. It has both good and bad sides to it. On one side a human being is so good as to be considered a creature of a benevolent god and on the other so miserable as to be considered a prisoner of a cruel demonic deity. Life is full of joy and full of sorrow; full of pleasure and full of pain; full of virtue and full of vice. There is probably no one in the world even among the healthiest and the wealthiest, who is not tormented sometime or other by fears and tensions. But in spite of that complexity of existence, according to the Hindu view, human life is not destined to annihilation or extinction. Hidden within the heart of every human being, there is a divine power that will eventually conquer evil, bring full liberation to the individual and lead it to dwell within the supreme divinity.

(2) The second point worth considering is the place Hindu people have given to the image of the goddess in their pantheon. In general, every god has a goddess as his wife or consort; and what is rather strange is that the female deity is shown as more powerful than the male deity. The life power of the god is contained in the goddess. Without the consort, any god is lifeless.

This could be a reflection of the esteem Indian people show to the woman both as spouse and mother. That reflection may go counter to the widespread opinion held about Indian society. The general impression diffused about Indian society is that it is one where women are disregarded and considered much lower in rank to men. But the deeper conviction of Indian people is what is portrayed in the goddess image. They look at the woman as the one on whom the survival and progress of society as also its spirituality depends.

(3) A final point to be given thought is the answer to the question: What is the secret power that has given unity to Hinduism? Hinduism is probably the oldest religion in the world, and the one followed by millions inhabiting one of the largest peninsulas of the world. It could well be also the only religion in the world with no uniformity in beliefs and practices.

But if a religion without uniformity in beliefs and practices has survived unbroken for so long, it is because Indian people have considered their motherland sacred to them. They have wanted to keep rooted in their land regardless of diversities in the form of worship, and even accepting differences in social patterns such as caste, class and family tradition. This firm attachment of the Indian people to their motherland is what has provided unity to Hinduism.

Chapter 4
Hinduism of the Modern Era

Among the numerically large religions of the modern world, there is not the least doubt, that Hinduism is certainly the oldest. The special characteristic of Hinduism is that it has survived all along in the same land in which it originated. It is not easy to understand how one religion could have survived for over thirty five centuries in a country like India, which is beset with endless problems, incongruities and hazards.

Of the problems Hinduism has had to face, quite a number are rooted in India itself. Of these the one that could be considered the most formidable is the caste system which divides society into different grades and classes. In an early era, the caste system was beneficial to society as it provided an automatic solution to the employment problem. Employments that society required were fixed by birth. But today employment requirements have changed but the caste system has remained unchanged. Today members of some classes do not even communicate with those of others.

A second abnormality is the lack of uniformity in the beliefs and practices of Hinduism itself. A third is the country's economic instability, which makes it impossible for millions of its population to satiate their day-to-day hunger.

The problems coming from outside the country are not less dreadful. Of these what the Hindus have found most difficult to face have been the invasions of Muslim and Western Christian powers. Not stopping with the acquirement of political control, the invading powers have tried to diffuse their religions within the country.

If Hinduism has not got crushed under obstacles as insurmountable as those, coming from both inside and outside the country, it is because it has enjoyed a mysterious inner strength which has kept it invincible. The source of that inner strength is no other than the inspiration given by the great sages and visionaries who appeared in Hindu society at every moment of crisis. These sages were called "Rishis". The Jews, who are members of probably the other oldest religion, would have called them "prophets".

The Rishis with their ingrained vision and insight could tell the Hindu community which direction they should take to overcome the crises. It is those Rishis who constructed the texts that constitute the sacred scriptures of Hinduism. From the number and the nature of

Building Bridges

those texts we can gauge the number and nature of the Rishis who have contributed to the unbroken survival and the continued growth of Hinduism. Therefore if we want to get some idea of the current state of Hinduism and the way it is moving, there is nothing better for us to do than to look speedily at a few of the Rishis of the last centuries. We give below a brief account of just five of them.

19. 1. Raja Ram Mohan (1772- 1833)

He was a Vaishnavite born to a devout Brahmin family. Because of the extra-ordinary contribution he made to the development of Hindu society he has been acclaimed as "the Father of Modern India". What he started with is somewhat unusual. He made a determined effort to understand the teachings of the other religions practiced in India. To understand religions like Islam and Christianity he went to the extent of learning the original languages of those religions such as Arabic, Persian, Hebrew and Greek. He encouraged everybody to respect the religions of others. He strongly upheld the view that the knowledge of the religions of others is vital for securing peace and harmony within the nation.

For the advancement of the Hindu community and very especially for the unification of the diverse forms of worship in the Hindu religion he created a monotheistic organization called the "Brahma–samaj" ("God-centered society"). The members of that association met together weekly to read and discuss Veda texts and to sing devotional Hindu songs. He was an expert in the English language. He strongly upheld that English should be the main second language of India.

20. 2. Dayananda Saraswathie Swami (1824-1883)

He was a Shaivite monk of the Gujarat Province. He too started a monotheistic organization. But to keep it more accessible to rural folk he called it the "Arya-samaj" or "nobility oriented society". Its motto was "Back to the Vedas". Till that time, ordinary people had no access to the Vedas and they were even forbidden to discuss it. The study of the Vedas was a privilege reserved for the Brahmin priestly caste. He opened the doors of the Vedas to members of all the different castes.

He shifted the attention of Hindu devotees from polytheism to monotheism. He strongly affirmed that India should give priority to science and technology so that the machinery for the development of India could be developed within the country itself. He was unshaken in his view that India could liberate itself from the narrow religious theologies and the technological devises of imperial powers only if it rose to the highest level in science and technology.

21. 3. Ramakrishna Paramahamsa (1834-1886)

Ramakrishna Paramahamsa who is today considered the most popular preacher of the teachings of the Veda, comes from a family of the Brahmin caste in Bengal. Since he had not received any higher education, he went to Calcutta for service in a temple dedicated to the goddess Kali. There he led a life of rigorous fast and extensive meditation. In course of those meditations he saw apparitions of goddess Kali and of other gods and goddesses. He had apparitions of Muhammad and Jesus too.

What he learnt from those apparitions he eventually started preaching. A dominant feature of his philosophy was that every Hindu should, while adhering to his own religion, have a deep respect for the teachings of all other religions. They should also adopt for their practice higher moral values taught by those religions. He came eventually to be venerated under the name of Shri Ramakrishna Paramahamsa.

22. 4. Vivekananda Swami (1862-1902)

He is the one who found a way to diffuse the teachings of Ramakrishna Paramahamsa throughout the world. By birth his name was Narendra Nath Dutt. Feeling unhappy with the polytheistic forms of Hindu worship prevailing in India of his day, he gave up god-belief altogether and became an atheist. But once he came to meet Shri Ramakrishna. He was so impressed by what he taught he became one of his disciples and became a monk taking the name of Vivekananda swami.

He realized that the essence of Hinduism was so profound and so universally valid that it deserved to be made known to everybody in modern society. With that aim in view he started an organization called the "Ramakrishna Mission". The key theme propagated by this mission is that everybody who genuinely adhered to Hinduism should respect the teachings of all other religions and observe the moral values contained in them.

The Ramakrishna mission became so popular that its branches began to spread not only in India but in almost every city of the modern world. The number of its branches in America is very large. The greatest glory of Vivekananda swami is that he spread out to the whole world the message of Hinduism which was till then restricted to the precincts of India.

23. 5. Mahatma Gandhi (1868-1848)

Though there are many other Hindu leaders who have contributed to the present state of India, and deserve to be mentioned here, we have room to mention only one more. We select Mahathma Gandhi. His full name is Mohandas Karamchand Gandhi. The epithet "Mahathma" which means "high souled" or "large hearted" was added to his name by people who venerated him. He belonged to the third Hindu caste called "Vaishya" which consisted of traders and businessmen. He studied law at the London University and thereafter went to Natal in South Africa to fight for the human rights of the Indians there. Later he returned to India to fight for its liberation from the political control of the British. After India gained independence, he was killed by an extremist of the political Hindu league.

Gandhi got all his strength for his political struggle from his religious philosophy. He made non-violence his chief weapon. His mind opened to the liberating power of non-violence as a result of his study of the teachings of Jainism, the Bhagavadgita, Jesus" Sermon on the Mount, and the teachings of Tolstoy.

He took great pains to do away with the caste system prevailing in Hindu society. He sought to raise the lot of the outcastes and untouchables by calling them "Harijans", "God's people". He led the Harijans into forbidden temples and got them the power to vote in political elections. He devised ways to destroy the poverty of village people. He taught rural folk to weave clothes on machines made of wood and forbade the import of foreign cloth into the country.

From a large number of visionary leaders from recent India, we have mentioned only five. But even from the thought patterns of that small number we can visualize the direction in which Hinduism is moving today. A few characteristics of that new direction may be summed up as follows.

Educated Hindus today are intent on wiping out the caste system from India. They are determined as well to liberate the village people from their poverty. To achieve that aim they have already developed an education system which gives prominence to science, technology, and the English language. With regard to the attitude to other religions, they have taken a stand which puts Hinduism far above all other religions. While adhering to their religion, they have undertaken to show an openness and respect to all religions of the world.

Because of such trends, Hinduism, which was so far restricted to one motherland, has started to receive an unprecedented welcome from people outside India. It is very likely that in course of time Hindu spirituality will become one of the most inspiring spiritualties of the world at large.

**World Religions
Part Two
Buddhism**

Chapter 1
A Religion With a Difference

Of the five religions dealt with in this book, it is not impossible that Buddhism would be the one that many will find strange and even intriguing. This is because, when they learn what the Buddha taught, they may be compelled to ask if Buddhism could be categorized as a religion. This is because god-belief is an integral part of what is commonly called "religion". Followers of practically all religions profess faith in one god or a number of gods and goddesses; and the beliefs they are expected to adhere to, are shown as revelations of one or another deity.

But the Buddha did not refer to God or a god in his teachings. This is not because he was atheistic or anti-theistic. If he did not speak of God or gods, it is because the concept of god did not enter his understanding of liberation. Liberation is what all religions are concerned with. Some refer to it as "salvation" or "redemption". But what distinguishes Buddhism from all other religions is what the Buddha wanted to redeem human beings from. In one word it is "suffering" (in Pali, "dukkha"). It is the key word on which Buddhism is founded.

Gauthama Siddhartha, that today we call the Buddha, was not a person who belonged to the ordinary rank and file of people. Ordinary people have endless hardships to bear up. Gauthama was a royal prince, son of a regional king. How such a person enjoying the comforts of a palace could have come to the conclusion that life is suffering and that every human being is born to suffer would no doubt be baffling to many.

There is no need to explain to anybody what suffering is. There is nobody who, if not suffering now, has not suffered before. Hunger, poverty, sickness in its hundreds of forms, passing away of a dear one, failure in undertakings, depressions and fears are some sufferings. Suffering is so universal that the general conviction of anybody is that suffering is inescapable and unavoidable.

The Buddha took those physical and mental sufferings of human beings into consideration and with the aim of finding a cure for suffering he searched for the root cause of suffering. He did not see the need to go to celestial or infernal beings to find out who or what caused suffering. He wanted to find the cause of suffering as also the solution to it from within the two-meter sized human being on earth.

But of that human being, he focused attention on the mental side than on the physical. He discovered that a sick disoriented mind was what caused suffering in its most painful and unbearable form. A well-rested and a rightly oriented mind made suffering painless and human life permanently peaceful. The Buddha was thus a mind-healer and a psychologist. What he taught the world was a mind-healing methodology. That is what makes it difficult for anybody to consider him as the founder of a religion. If Buddhism is treated as a religion, it will have to be categorized not as a "theistic religion" but as a "secular religion" or an "experiential religion".

24. Diverse Forms of Buddhism Today

To understand what the Buddha taught we have naturally to go beyond Buddhism of the diverse forms in which it is found today. Like all other major religions in the modern world, Buddhism too consists of culturally distinct traditions. Those divisions however are not difficult to recognize. Of these, the two considered oldest are the Theravāda [1] (in Pāli, "the Tradition of the Elders") and the Mahayāna (Sanskrit for "Larger Vehicle").

The Theravāda adheres to the teachings of the early monastic writings and upholds, to a large extent, that salvation is the prerogative of monks. The Mahayāna is more liberal and upholds that anyone whether monk or lay, male or female has the ability to attain salvation of the highest form.

The Theravāda tradition is followed today in countries like Sri Lanka, Myanmar (former Burma) Thailand, Cambodia, Laos and Malaysia; and Mahayāna in countries like Tibet, China, Korea, Japan, and Vietnam. Of the schools that developed later the more prominent are Ch'an (Zen), Lamaism, Tendai, Nichiren, and Soko Gakkai.

Hardly any of the institutional versions of contemporary Buddhism are of a non-theistic form. They have all absorbed the theistic patterns of religions prevailing in their regions. The Theravada Buddhists of Sri Lanka, for example, worship gods and goddesses of the Hindu pantheon. It is difficult to find any Theravada shrine to which a Hindu temple is not attached.

---

[1] Please note: The long sounding vowels of Pāli and Sanskrit words are underlined in the English words given in this book, v.g. Theravāda, Mahayāna

The only complete canon of the Buddhist scriptures is the Tri-pitaka (literally "Three Baskets") written in Pali. Though the books of the Tripitaka are found, wholly or in part, also in other languages such as Sanskrit and Chinese, the Tripitaka of the Pali tradition is what is considered the oldest. Those of the Mahayana tradition too respect them though they give priority to their own books such as the "Lotus Sutra" and the "Lalita-vistara". We will be resorting mainly to the Pali Tri-pitaka in our study of Buddhism here.[2]

The multiplicity of the versions of Buddhism is not a serious obstacle to finding out what Buddhism was in its original form. To overcome that obstacle all that we have to do is to take the trouble to examine the earliest scriptural writings. In the Buddhist scriptures, what the Buddha taught is clearly contained in his first and foremost sermon called the sermon of "the Four Noble Truths". It is that sermon that we will be taking into consideration here.

25. Value of Buddhism to Non-Buddhists

As said earlier, the Buddha had no other intention than to discover an effective psychology to heal human beings of their inner suffering. However astounding it may sound, that approach has been found to be greatly appealing to people of other religions, especially to theistic, and very especially monotheistic religions. What leads me to that conclusion is something that happened to a little book I wrote on Buddhism. I wrote that book when I was teaching Buddhism to the students of a Christian Seminary. What I included in the book was what I taught them in class.

The book was titled *"Buddhism and Christianity, their Inner Affinity"*. The book consisted of two parts. In the first, I explained Buddha's teaching on the Eightfold Path. In the second I tried to show that what Buddhists were expected to acquire through Mental Enlightenment was not very different from the peace of mind that Christians were expected to achieve through submission to the will of God.

The book was well received, and by a strange combination of circumstances, not long after it was locally published, it got into the hands of one Dr. Leonard Swidler, an American scholar of World

---

[2] Please note: The long sounding vowels of Pali and Sanskrit words are underlined in the English words given in this book, v.g. Theravada, Mahayana

Religions. He came to see me saying that this book made good sense to Christians and if he was given permission he could add a few paragraphs to make it useful to another group of monotheists, the Jews. I did not hesitate to give the permission.

The title he gave to the new edition was *"Buddhism Made Plain: An exposition for Christians and Jews"* (by Antony Fernando with Leonard Swidler). The book was published by iPub Global Connection and Orbis, New York, and up to date it has been printed nine times. It was printed in India too, and has since then been translated into other languages such as Italian, French, German, Spanish and Burmese. This is what made me suspect that, if rightly understood, Buddhism could be of interest to non-Buddhists too.

Since it is primarily a mind-healing methodology, even theists such as Jews, Christians and Muslims could benefit from Buddhism to keep their minds rightly oriented and be cured of mind-tormenting ailments such as depressions, fears and tensions which are actually the sufferings most difficult to live with.

Chapter 2
Life and Personality of the Buddha

The best introduction to the philosophy of great persons is their own life, for events in their life are generally connected with developments in their thought. This is no less true of Gautama the Buddha and his philosophy.

Unfortunately for us, we know only very little of the Buddha's own life. He lived twenty five hundred years ago, or five hundred years before Christ, and the little we know of him from the scriptures may not be historical in every detail. Certain facts contained in the scriptures seem to have been intentionally fitted in by redactors to bring out the particular role he played as the founder of Buddhism.

Such uncertainty in biographical details is not a weakness peculiar to the Buddhist scriptures. As any Bible student today knows only too well, we cannot build a strictly historical account of Christ's life from the Gospel narratives. Their authors, for example, were not preoccupied, as we are today, with the need for recording a diary account of Christ's life and activity. They narrate events of his life only as necessary for their purpose which was religious instruction. Thus what the Gospels have preserved for us are educational rather than historical accounts of the life of Christ.

The Buddha's life story seems to be arranged with a similar purpose, – namely, to make his teachings more acceptable and more meaningful. As far as we are concerned, that does not matter, because thereby his biography becomes a kind of commentary on his teaching. The scriptural account of the Buddha's life, therefore is worthy of serious study.

26. Home Life

To begin with, it is useful to keep in mind that the term "Buddha" is an honorary title attributed to him, very much like the name "Christ" given to Jesus. His family name was Gautama, his personal name Siddhartha.

Siddhartha Gautama was born in a materially well-to-do family. His father was chief of a clan called the Sakyans, on the Nepalese frontier, in a region called Kapilavastu. There were many such chiefs in the same kingdom. His mother Mahamaya, was a princess of the Kolian clan. The fact that the father of Gautama was a civic chief is important. It means that Gautama belonged not to the Brahmin or the priestly caste, but to the kshatriya or the soldier caste. Had he belonged by birth to the Brahmin caste, traditionally pre-occupied with rites and rituals, gods and goddesses, it would not have been easy for him to found a religion in which the God-concept would be absent.

The birth of Gautama took place outside his home, while his mother was on a journey. She was on her way from Kapilavastu to her parental home in Devadaha. In India, a woman goes to her mother for the delivery of the first baby, which probably is the reason for the journey Mahamaya had undertaken. Gauthama Siddhartha was born in the park of Lumbini under the shade of a Sal tree.

According to a virgin-birth legend found in certain books of the Mahayana tradition, Gautama came into the world from the side of his mother, without causing her any pain, while she was holding a branch of the tree. Mahamaya died on the seventh day, so Gautama missed the tender care of his mother. He was reared by his mother's sister, Prajapathi Gotami.

His education, in keeping with the family traditions of the kshatriya or soldier-caste was necessarily a very good one. Like all other noblemen, he would have been well-trained in archery and the art of war.

Marriage in India is an event that is woven into an intricate tradition. We do not know anything about the background of Gauthama's marriage, except that he married his cousin Yasodhara at the age of sixteen. She was the only daughter of King Suppabuddha. They had one son named Rahula.

27. Renunciation

Gautama's father had great plans for his son; he wished for him a glamorous political carrier. To encourage him towards such a goal, he tried to provide his son with many luxuries. It is said that he took special precautions to keep the miseries of life from his son's inquiring eyes. His efforts were not successful, for reality can never escape a person who is alert. Gautama did see the reality of life, and his sight or insight was powerful enough to bring an altogether new turn in his life.

Life and Personality of the Buddha

Gautama's understanding of the reality of life, which was the prelude to his first major decision about his career, is traditionally presented as four visions. They are:
1. A man weakened with age,
2. A sick man with infested skin and bones,
3. A dead man being taken into the cemetery,
4. A recluse with a calm and serene face.

Of these four scenes, the first three fall into one category and the fourth into another. The first three show facets of the reality of ailing humanity. The last shows one possible relief from it.

These four visions, if rightly understood could give us a correct insight into the doctrine that he later taught. He taught a way of escaping the suffering caused by old age, sickness, and death. The way is the life of renunciation. Of course, as everybody knows, even a monk who renounces the world does not escape sickness, old age, and death. But he does escape the agony caused by them in as much as his mind is not unduly attached to transient aspects of life, and he does not consider transient realities to be ultimate values.

This shocking discovery of the transitory nature of life, and the subsequent folly of being attracted by transitory values, caused Gautama to decide to renounce the world and become an ascetic. He was twenty nine years of age when he took this step. He was no longer a teen-ager, having behind him already thirteen ears of married life. The decision taken at such an age must be viewed as one which is well-considered and mature.

A modern person may be somewhat shocked at the idea of a married person leaving his wife and child behind to enter the monastic life. We must view such happenings in the light of the social traditions prevalent at the time. Leaving home for the practice of asceticism after a period of married life was an approved form of behavior in Hindu society. According to the Hindu ideal, a person aspiring to perfection had to organize his life in a certain gradation. He had first to be a celibate student, then a married man, and finally either an ascetic or a hermit. According to that commonly accepted tradition, Gautama's behavior was not at all abnormal.

Further, if the Indian family system is taken into account, where a strong sense of unity prevails among relatives, leaving behind a wife and child did not amount to abandonment. They were always taken care of by the parents, parents-in-law, or uncles and aunts. Even though he renounced family life in keeping with an existing tradition, what is important for us to realize is that he did not follow that tradition blindly. That is where the particular greatness of Gautama's decision lies.

He was bold enough to challenge the notion of renunciation and religion itself. He was sharp enough to suspect that, just as much as life in the world, life as a hermit or an ascetic too could itself be a trap. That is why the scriptures do not say that he left home just to become an ascetic or a monk. According to the Buddhist scriptures he left family life "in quest of the supreme security from bondage in quest of Nibbana (Nirvana)".[1]

28. Search

His first experiment was with systems of meditation. He placed himself under the guidance of two well-known yogi teachers of the time, Alara Kalama and Uddhaka Rama Putta. It is very likely that Gautama profited from this training in yoga, and that he acquired from his teachers a facility in meditation. But Gautama did not attach an all-inclusive importance to the techniques of yoga, nor did he look approvingly at the pre-occupation of these yogi teachers with the meditational status known as "trances".

Meditation, to be sure, is a very important feature in Buddhism, but Gautama was not interested in meditation simply for the sake of meditation. For Gautama, the right type of meditation had to lead an individual not just to an ephemeral experience but to an *insight* into the deeper realities of life. The type of meditation he later undertook to promote is a system of meditation called "Insight Meditation" (Vipassana-Bhavana).

"Insight" is a power of knowledge far superior to "reason" which provides the basis for physical sciences. Reason can't lead to religion. Exponents of theistic religions explain "insight" as an outpouring of "divine revelation".

The second stage of his search consisted of an experiment with asceticism. After leaving the yogi teachers, Gautama joined a hermitage or "ashram" in which five ascetics are said to have lived together. Such ashrams were common in the India of Gautama's day. This particular hermitage was situated in Uruwela by the river Neranjala at Gaya. The names of the five ascetics, as preserved for us

---

[1] MN. 1, 163, sutta 26

in the scriptures, are Kondanna, Bhaddiya, Vappa, Mahanama and Assaji.

These monks practiced the strictest asceticism. They believed that self-mortification and self-torture had in them a liberating power. Even in modern India, it is not uncommon to find ascetics and even lay persons who believe in that philosophy. At certain penitential shrines, penitents can be seen sticking themselves with hooks, cutting themselves with blades and spikes, rolling on hot sand, walking on nailed shoes, and the like.

These monks believed mainly in fasts, living exclusively on leaves and roots. Gautama followed those disciplines so vigorously that the absolute paucity of nourishment left him a physical wreck. Describing the emaciated state of his body that resulted from it, he said:

"Rigorous have I been in my ascetical discipline. Rigorous have I been beyond all others; like wasted, withered reeds became all my limbs".[2]

It was not long, before he realized the utter futility of such self-mortification to achieve liberation. He soon saw that what is required for liberation is not self-mortification but self-discipline or self-mastery. As soon as he discovered that pure asceticism could not give the deeper form of mental liberation he sought after, he waved his companions good-bye and began to pursue his search all by himself.

The period of search under yogi teachers and with ascetics is mentioned in the scriptures as having lasted six years. There are two important facts about Gautama's personality that stand out from the period of his search.

First, it shows, without any doubt, that Gautama had a very strong spirit of determination. Six years is a long period and any ordinary person could have given up or been satisfied with an easier solution. He was also very sincere in whatever he did. Whether it was meditation or asceticism, he practiced with the full devotion of his heart and soul. All that indicates clearly, that he had a mind of his own. He did not accept tradition or authority without judgment and so, was able to disagree with traditions and teachers.

Secondly, this period of experimentation shows a clear evolution of his convictions. A very clear element of his philosophy is the uncompromising rejection of asceticism. His system was called a

---

[2] MN.1, 246, sutta 26

"Middle Path" primarily because he wanted to declare himself against asceticism in its physical and external form. He considered such asceticism just as harmful to human perfection as self-indulgence.

29. Discovery Through Enlightenment

After leaving the ascetical school, Gautama continued his search, reflecting on liberation and the path to it in total solitude. Under a large shady tree, which eventually came to be called the "Bodhi Tree" (in short, "Bo-tree" and literally, the "Tree of Enlightenment" or "of Wisdom") he meditated on his past life and on the un-liberated state of the lives of others. He sought the reasons that keep men and women in an un-liberated state and there he discovered the real nature of human suffering, the cause of it, the ability to escape from it, and the path for such an escape. It is this discovery that is referred to by the technical term "Enlightenment (Bodhi)".

He saw the reality of human suffering and the possibility of human joy in a way that he had never seen before. His conviction was such that he realized, once and for all, the path to true joy of existence. The conviction was so powerful that with it he felt a sense of mission to preach it to the whole world. A God-believer would have expressed this discovery, in the language proper to him as "revelation". But for Gautama it was something that "arose" from within himself as a result of his personal concentration. He expressed this experience of "enlightenment" in a spirit of joy and humility.

Being myself subject to birth, ageing, decease, death, sorrow, and defilement, seeing danger in what is subject to these things, seeking the unborn, un-ageing, decease-less, death-less, sorrow-less, un-defiled, supreme security from bondage – Nirvana, I attained it. Knowledge and vision arose in me. Unshakeable is my deliverance of mind.[3]

Gautama was so enraptured by his discovery that he spent seven weeks in meditation in the same area and one entire week looking with immense gratitude at the tree that shaded him. This shows the magnitude of his sense of discovery. Though in an entirely different field, the "Eureka" feeling that he experienced could not have differed from the feeling that in a later era Isaac Newton experienced when he discovered gravity, Pasteur, germs, and Columbus, America.

---

[3] MN.1, 166, sutta 26

30. Nirvana as Liberation

In the above statement, the Buddha used the word "Nirvana" to express the state of relief he experienced after bringing sorrow and suffering to a termination. "Nirvana" is a word that is close in meaning to "undisturbed mental rest". To clarify that liberated state of existence (in the quotation above) he has used the words "the unborn, un-ageing, decease-less, death-less, sorrow-less, un-defiled, supreme security from bondage". To understand those words meaningfully we must take them in parallel with the words he used (in the same statement) to describe the un-liberated state which are "being subject to birth, ageing, decease, death, sorrow, and defilement." As we will see better when we examine the Sermon of the Four Noble Truths, the difference between the "un-liberated" and the "liberated" is the same as between the "sorrowful passionate life" and the "sorrow-less dispassionate life".

The great discovery of the Buddha was that every human being is born with a disoriented state of mind. Because of that disorientation nobody endowed with senses can avoid passionately yearning for pleasure and possessions. That yearning is what causes sorrow. But the Buddha also discovered that this mental disorientation could be corrected and that the passionate thirst for material wellbeing can be overcome. The dispassionate person comes to a state where his or her mind is completely restful and permanently joyful.

But what would intrigue a non-Buddhist is that the Buddha does not say anything about Nirvana except that it is a sorrow-less dispassionate level of life. Just like the Buddha, anybody can achieve that level of life on earth itself. But the Buddha does not say anything about life after death. That is not because he denies it, but like any other scientist he does not want to discuss the non-physical aspects of life. Non-physical realities are invisible and so, except through pictures, inexpressible in day-to-day language. That is why he did not want to speak of God too.

In all religions divinity as also life after-death have been picturized. Divinity has been shown as celestial beings and life after death as a living in heaven or in the residence of god. The Buddha abstained from picturization. He left the reality of realization to be experienced or seen by one's own insight. But what the Buddha implied, and has left unsaid, can be suspected. He described Nirvana as "deathless" which in other religions will be equal to "eternal".

31. Preaching the Message

The Buddha started his preaching mission with those he had known before. The first group he approached was the five ascetics with whom he had lived. His sense of friendship was such that he did not reject them as individuals, even though he rejected their philosophy. He wanted to share with them his newly-won insight into liberation and travelled one hundred and fifty miles to meet them.

When he first spoke to them, they did not attach any importance to his views but, like any great person, the Buddha knew how to convert them to him by the very simplicity of his approach. He asked them, "Have I ever spoken to you like this, as one who claimed to know the truth?" This simple appeal appeared irresistible to them. When they were ready to listen he started the exposition of his new system of liberation which he termed the "Middle Path".

These five monks became his first followers and the first members of the monastic order that he established. Soon afterwards, the Vinaya Pitaka says a group of fifty five young lay persons joined the order. Many others followed suit and the order grew very rapidly.

The Buddha established a monastic order for women as well. But admission into the orders of the monks or the nuns was not the only way of gaining discipleship under the Buddha. Lay persons too were accepted as disciples. The sermon called the Maha Vacca Gotta Sutta[4] indicates that a large lay discipleship consisting of men and women, married and unmarried formed as great a part of the Buddha's organization as did monks and nuns. The Buddha clearly affirmed that full liberation was also within their reach.

One of the special functions of the monks was that of preaching the doctrine. Buddhism from the beginning was missionary in outlook. The formula the Buddha used in sending out the first group of missionaries shows clearly the nature and aim of Buddhist missionary work.

"Delivered am I, monks, from all forms of mental slavery; you also are delivered. Go now, and wonder for the welfare and happiness of the many out of compassion for the world, for the gain, welfare, and happiness of the entire universe. Let not two of you proceed in the same direction. Proclaim the Dhamma (the way to liberation), that is so excellent, so meaningful and so perfect. Proclaim the life of

---
[4] MN. 1, 490 -91

purity, the holy life, consummate and pure. There are beings with a little dust in their eyes, who will be lost through not learning the Dhamma. There are beings who will understand Dhamma[5].

The missionary activity of the order was crowned with great success in Buddha's own time. The secret of success was simply the relevance of the doctrine he preached; at a time when ideas of religion and liberation were so confused he presented a purified view of religion and liberation that was easy to understand and precise enough to follow.

This, of course, does not mean that the Buddha did not have his own problems and setbacks. One of his greatest sufferings could well have been the opposition to his leadership in the order that was fostered by a monk called Devadatta, who was also a cousin of his. The latter struggled very hard to take over the leadership of the order. The difficulties that the Buddha experienced in such matters were so great that at times he went into long retreats in the forest to escape from them.

32. The Super-humanity of the Buddha

We cannot conclude the story of this great religious leader without a word concerning his personal sanctity. According to the Buddha there were four basic qualities that were to characterize any Buddhist saint or liberated person. They are:

1. *Metta* - Friendliness or loving kindness
2. *Karuna* - Compassion
3. *Mudhita* - Gentleness
4. *Upekkha* - Equanimity

These four qualities that he recommended to others were also qualities that he practiced himself. One little incident shows how seriously he practiced such virtues in his own life. As the order grew and established itself in distant places, he made it a point to visit groups of monks residing in different areas and assure himself of their welfare.

One monastery he so visited, had a monk who was very ill. The monk was suffering from an advanced skin disease. The eczema had spread so much that his entire body seemed one single sore. Blood and pus oozed out to the extent that his clothes were stuck to his body.

---

[5] VP – MV. 21, i, 11: 1

His companions, because of the filthiness of his state had kept aloof and abandoned him to endure his misfortune alone.

The Buddha visited this monk in the company of his close associate Ananda. Then, taking a basin of water and a towel, he washed the patient himself and cleaned him. After doing whatever was possible to bring relief to him, he walked down to the little hut of the other monks. He inquired from them about the sick monk and why they neglected to look after him. Their reply was that, in as much as he was certain to die, he was of no benefit to the order. Then, with the intention of opening their eyes to the heartlessness of such behavior, the Buddha said,

"Monks, you do not have a mother, you do not have a father here who can tend you; if you, monks, do not tend one another, who is there to tend you? Remember that whoever tends a sick person, as it were, tends me."[6]

The Buddha thus showed himself to be a person who practiced the virtues he preached. The Buddha lived up to the age of eighty. His death occurred at Kusinara one hundred and twenty miles from Benares in what is now Uttara Pradesh. The last words he addressed to his assembled disciples are very significant. "Passionate life is transient; achieve well-being with effort and mental alertness".

Thus the need for effort and for attentiveness to right life-values was stressed during his last moment on earth as it had been throughout his life. Even though his life ended twenty five hundred years ago this message of his continues to live on even in our day.

---

[6] VP-MV, 302 viii, 26:3

Chapter 3
The Sermon of the Four Noble Truths

The sermon of the Four Noble Truths is the best and safest text to be made use of when trying to understand the philosophy of the Buddha. It is his very first sermon, and the one that is universally accepted as the clearest summary of all that he taught and stood for. Since it is this text that will have to form the core of our investigation it is only appropriate that we have an idea of the full text as given in the scriptures. We take it from the Vinaya Pitaka.

So as to make it easier to follow the sequence of thought in it, the text is here divided into three parts marked A, B, C. In the central part (B), the Buddha expounds, through the Four Noble Truth, his stand on the way to liberation from mental suffering. The first Part (A) is a prelude and the third part (C) a conclusion. Since the focus of attention of the sermon is the Eightfold Path it is here presented in Italics. The Eightfold Path is repeated three times in the text.

33. Text of Sermon

(A) These two extremes, monks, are not to be approached by him who has withdrawn from the world. Which two? One is that which is linked and connected with lust, through sensuous pleasures, because it is low, of the uncultured, of the mediocre man, ignoble and profitless. The other is that which is connected with mortification and asceticism, because it is painful, and incapable of achieving the target.

Avoiding both these extremes, monks, take the Middle Path, which brings insight, brings knowledge, and leads to tranquility, to full knowledge to full enlightenment, to Nirvāna, which is the Eightfold Path, namely, *1. Right View, 2. Right Resolve, 3. Right Speech, 4. Right Action, 5. Right Livelihood, 6. Right Effort, 7. Right Mindfulness, and 8. Right Insight-Meditation.* It is this which brings insight, brings knowledge and leads to tranquility, to highest awareness to full enlightenment, to Nirvāna.

And monks, what is this Middle Path that leads to Nirvāna? It is indeed, the Noble Eightfold Path, namely, *1. Right View, 2. Right Resolve, 3. Right Speech, 4. Right Action, 5. Right Livelihood, 6. Right Effort, 7. Right Mindfulness, and 8. Right Insight-Meditation.* The Middle Path leads to Nirvāna.

(B) Now, monks, this is the Noble Truth as to sorrow. Birth (earthly existence) indeed is sorrowful. Disease, death, union with the unpleasing, separation from the pleasing is sorrowful; in brief, desirous, transient individuality (carnal existence) is sorrowful.

Again monks, this is the Noble Truth as to the origin of sorrow. It is the recurring greed, associated with enjoyment and desire and seeking pleasure everywhere, which is the cause of this sorrow, in other words, it is the greed for sense pleasure, greed for carnal existence, and the greed for possessions.

Again, monks, this is the Noble Truth as to the cessation of sorrow. It is the complete cessation, giving up, abandoning, release and detachment from greed.

And this once more, monks, is the Noble Truth as to the path to the cessation of sorrow. It is indeed that Noble Eightfold Path: *1. Right View, 2. Right Resolve, 3. Right Speech, 4. Right Action, 5. Right Livelihood, 6. Right Effort, 7. Right Mindfulness, and 8. Right Insight-Meditation.* The Middle Path, monks, leads to Nirv<u>a</u>na.

(C) As soon, monks, as my knowledge and sight concerning these four Noble Truths became complete; I knew that I had attained supreme and full enlightenment. I became aware and fully convinced that my mind was liberated, that existence in its unhappy form had ended, and that there would no longer be an unhappy survival.

Thus spoke the Blessed One. The five monks, rejoicing, welcomed the word of the Blessed One.[1]

Even though this is probably the most important sermon of the Buddha, it is very unlikely that a reader will find its message self-evident. This is due to no fault of the reader, or even of the text. Ancient texts in any field of knowledge are not as easy to grasp as modern writings. The text goes back to over twenty five hundred years. To get at the crux of the sermon, we should keep in mind that it was preached to a group of five monks who upheld that body-tormenting asceticism was the only way to spiritual liberation.

34. Prelude and Conclusion

The prelude given in the first part (A) clarifies what the Buddha hoped to achieve through the sermon. His aim was to prove that a right-oriented mind was enough to achieve the liberation from

---

[1] VP.MV. 10, i, 6:17-23

suffering that everybody sought after. And the way to achieve that right orientation of mind was the practice of eight good day-to-day actions which taken together could be called the Eightfold Path. The specialty of the Eightfold Path was that it could be called a Middle Path because it avoided the two extremes of sensuousness and asceticism.

In the conclusion given in the final part (C), the Buddha affirms that there is no better proof for the validity of the Eightfold Path than his own experience. It was the practice of the Eightfold Path that led him to enlightenment and along with it an unshakable peace of mind.

35. Main Argument: Four Noble Truths

The main part of the sermon contained in section (B) is actually a well prepared logical argument. It consists of four paragraphs. The first three are the premises, the last the conclusion deriving from the premises. The content of each paragraph is referred to as a "Noble Truth".

36. First Noble Truth

However ancient the text be, the first premise of the argument couldn't have been worded better. In it he makes specific the particular peril he wants to liberate human beings from. There are of course numerous types of peril from which human beings seek redemption. One, for example is political. People controlled by a tyrant seek for redemption from slavery under him. Another is physical. A pestilence, famine or a lasting drought are such. A third which is particular to religions is sin and sinfulness which is said to bring people under the sway of infernal forces. But the peril that the Buddha focused attention on is special. What people need liberation from mostly is the emotional disorder in their minds because this is what causes immense mental suffering.

Now, monks, this is the Noble Truth as to sorrow. Birth (carnal existence) indeed is sorrowful. Disease, death, union with the unpleasing, separation from the pleasing is sorrowful; in brief, desirous, transient individuality (carnal existence) is sorrowful.

Sorrowfulness is a reality that, however widespread it be, is not easy to explain. But a fundamental fact of life is that people suffer more deeply from depression, disheartenment, rejection, lovelessness, jealousy, hatred, anger, possessiveness and fear of people and failure, than for instance, from hunger or poverty. Anybody sincere enough to look into one's own heart can in no way escape that fact.

37. Second Noble Truth

The first Noble Truth implies that, however universal this particular type of suffering be it is in no way invincible. But for it to become remediable, we must know where the suffering operates and how it originates. This is what is brought out in the second Noble Truth. Suffering is caused by a misguided mind to yearn for earthly pleasures.

Again, monks, this is the Noble Truth as to the origin of sorrow. It is the recurring greed, associated with enjoyment and desire and seeking pleasure everywhere, which is the cause of this sorrow, in other words, it is the greed for sense pleasure, greed for carnal existence, and the greed for possessions.

There is no difficulty in understanding that statement. The cause of inner suffering is greed or the thirst to satisfy one's emotional desires. In the expression "greed for carnal existence", the Pali word translated as "existence" is "bhava" and refers not to existence of the general sense but to existence of the passionate form filled with sense desires.

Thus, the real source of suffering is the endless search for emotional fulfillment which is inevitable because of the disoriented state of a person's mind. That disorientation of mind is what everybody is born with and usually lives with.

38. Third Noble Truth

The third truth is linked with the first and the second and flows automatically from them.

Again, monks, this is the Noble Truth as to the cessation of sorrow. It is the complete cessation, giving up, abandoning, release and detachment from greed.

This statement leaves no doubt as to what constitutes liberation from mental suffering. If mental suffering is due to thirst for carnal satisfaction, and that thirst is due to a disoriented mind, then the path to liberation is clear. The mind must be corrected so that it acts less emotionally and more insightfully. Then attachment to pleasure and possessions will pass away and the new spirit of detachment will bring with it lasting mental peace.

It is to emphasize what leads to mental peace that the Buddha here uses five expressions identical in meaning: "cessation of greed, giving up of greed, abandoning of greed, release from greed, and detachment from greed". Often he used the term "Nirvana" (Nibbana) to indicate the relief-full state of mind of the liberated person. As he says in the Anguttara Nikaya "Destruction of greed, greedless-ness, eradication of greed, that is Nirvana".[2]

"Nirvana", which today many ordinary people find difficult to understand, is not the only term that the Buddha used to designate the sublime state of happiness of the liberated individual. Nor is it even the word that he used most. In the book "Sutta Nipatha" the word "Nibbana" is used only fourteen times, whereas the word "Shanthi" which means "peace of mind" is used twenty nine times. "Nirvana" or "Shanthi" is thus a sublime state of mind realizable here and now.

39. Fourth Noble Truth

If the first three Noble Truths are considered the premises, the fourth is just the conclusion of the argument. For liberation from sorrow one does not have to resort to self-tormenting exercises. Nor is help from a supra-earthly power needed. The mind of each person is powerful enough to drive away emotional desires, and make the individual act insightfully. The purpose of the fourth Noble truth is to show what the right steps are that are needed to train one's mind to act insightfully.

And this once more, monks, is the Noble Truth as to the path to the cessation of sorrow. It is that Noble Eightfold Path: *1. Right View, 2. Right Resolve, 3. Right Speech, 4. Right Action, 5. Right Livelihood, 6. Right Effort, 7. Right Mindfulness, and 8. Right Insight-Meditation.* The Middle Path, monks, leads to Nirvana.

The explanation of the Four Noble Truths given above is brief. But it should be sufficient to make anyone discover the unusual message that the Buddha wanted to convey through them. He used the argument of the first three Truths to prove that the conclusion contained in the Fourth Truth, namely the Eightfold Path is the right way to relieve human beings of the inner suffering they are victims of.

---

[2] AN. 11, 34

In other words what he underlines is that the problem of suffering is a psychological problem. The sickness is in the mind and so is the cure. The Buddha is thus a psychologist whose sole purpose was to heal people of their psychological disorders. To understand this fact more clearly we should examine the steps of the Eightfold Path separately and also try to discover why he was led to call the Eightfold Path the "Middle Path".

Chapter 4
The Eightfold Path

Of the numerous paths to human liberation presented by different religions, the one proposed by the Buddha could well be the clearest and the shortest. It states clearly what the malady is, where it is rooted and how it is to be remedied. All are in the realm of the mind.

The remedy recommended is equally short. It consists of eight day-to-day duties to be performed with a pure mind. He expressed them in just eight words, or sixteen if we take them with word "right" (samma) attached in front of each. The word "right" indicates that any human activity can be done in both a right and wrong way.

The eight steps given in the Eightfold Path are: *1. Right View, 2. Right Resolve, 3. Right Speech, 4. Right Action, 5. Right Livelihood, 6. Right Effort, 7. Right Mindfulness, and 8. Right Insight-Meditation.* Here we will look at them one by one, and thereafter examine why the Buddha called the "Eightfold Path" the "Middle Path". The steps are named below, along with their Pali equivalents.

40. Steps of the Eightfold Path
41. 1. Right View of Life (samma ditthi)

The most important requirement for a human being to overcome suffering and live a life of peace and contentment is an insightful view of life and reality. The biggest obstacle to a life of peace and happiness is ignorance (avidya) of the right values of life. A mind can act selfishly or selflessly. A selfish or self-centered person does not realize that by trying to appease his pleasure-seeking senses, his life becomes transient (anicca), sorrowful (dukkha) and un-substantial (anatta). The selfless person is different. He is enlightened and so is aware of the right values of life. He is not possessive of anything or anybody. He is concerned about the welfare of others. He is compassionate and shows friendliness to everybody.

Buddha's greatest personal achievement was "enlightenment" or the understanding of the right values of life. That is what made it possible for him to distinguish between self-centered activities that make a person's life ignoble and sorrowful and reality-centered activities that make anyone's life noble and joyful. That is why he named "Right view of life" as the first step of the Eightfold Path.

42. 2. Right Resolve (samma sankappa)

The second step is, as it were, inseparable from the first. To act according to what one sees as right, calls for resolve and determination. On one side, a strong resolve is necessary to empty the mind of vices such as jealousy, anger, revenge and thirst for pleasure and on the other, a strong determination is indispensable to fill it with feelings of love, compassion and courage.

43. 3. Right Speech (samma vaca)

Speech is an activity anybody has to engage in during a large part of the day. But there is both a right and wrong way of speaking. Lies, gossip, tale-bearing, harsh words and the like form wrong speech. Giving educational information, saying encouraging and peace-promoting words and the like form right speech. Speech portrays the selfish and selfless states of a person's mind.

44. 4. Right Action (samma kammantha)

There are both good and bad actions that an individual can perform in one's day-to-day life. Among bad actions are, misappropriation of others' goods, destroying life, breaking up families, and wrong sexual behavior. Among good actions are helping the needy, protecting children and the aged, and promoting good will among people of different castes and creeds.

45. 5. Right Livelihood (samma ajiva)

Right livelihood is an item that any modern student of Buddhism should give special attention to, because that is one ignored or even played down by members of the monastic Theravada tradition.

The inclusion of Right Livelihood is a clear proof that the Buddha was not restricting his path to liberation to just the monks. Monks do not have to engage in a livelihood or a job to find their food. The laity provides it as alms to them. Therefore, the inclusion of Right Livelihood as an item of the Eightfold Path is a clear sign that for the Buddha the Eightfold Path was more for lay people than for monks.

For lay people there is both a right and a wrong way to do a job and earn one's livelihood. The proper way to make money is by rendering a genuine service to individuals. For a trader, on the other side, to earn money by selling things like drugs, weapons and outdated goods is wrong.

46. 6. Right Effort (samma vayama)

For any undertaking to be fruitful a serious effort is necessary and it must be maintained continuously. That effort is particularly necessary when the undertaking is of the mental order. To maintain an understanding of right life-values and to preserve that enlightenment till the end of life is not easy without sustained effort. To engage in right activities throughout one's life a great effort is necessary. Laziness is a hindrance to progress.

47. 7. Right Mindfulness (samma sati)

Another great obstacle to success in any undertaking is lack of attentiveness to the task one is engaged in. The tendency of most people is to be dreaming of some other thing when they are engaged in one activity. To overcome mental suffering one must constantly keep an eye on the circumstances that give rise to wrong emotional desires and know how to avoid the circumstances.

48. 8. Right Insight-Meditation (samma samadhi)

The Buddha valued meditation only for two targets that it was capable of achieving. One is to get the mind rested when it is fatigued. The exercise he recommended for it was that of restfully inhaling and exhaling one's breath for a while or just a few minutes. He called it "mind resting meditation" (samatha).

The other was not an exercise as such but an attitude to be maintained all through life. That attitude was one of insightfulness. He called it "insight meditation" (vipassana). He rejected totally the yogi systems of meditation because they were a burden to the mind. He had experimented with them himself and found them to be of no use for the cause of mental liberation.

One good way to get a clear idea of Buddha's attitude to meditation is to read the advice on meditation he gave his own son,

Venerable Rahula. The advice enumerates the principal types of meditation that are specifically Buddhist in character.

Develop the meditation on loving kindness (metta), Rahula, for by this ill-will is banished.

Develop the meditation on compassion, (karuna) Rahula, for by this cruelty is banished.

Develop the meditation on gentleness (mudhita), Rahula, for by this hard-heartedness is banished.

Develop the meditation on equanimity (upekkha), Rahula, for by this anxiety is banished.

Develop the meditation on the corruptibility of the body, (asubha), Rahula, for by this lust is banished.

Develop the meditation on impermanence (anicca), Rahula for by this the pride of self (Asmi-mana) is banished.

Develop the concentration of mindfulness by restful in and out breathing (ana-pana sati) Rahula, for this, if frequently practiced bears much fruit and is of great advantage.[1]

The exposition on Right Mediation concludes our study of the Eightfold Path. The Eightfold Path, contained in the fourth Noble Truth is what we could call the over-all essence of Buddha's teaching.

49. Revolutionary Nature of the Eightfold Path

As anybody will see if we express more succinctly what the Buddha taught through the Eightfold Path, it would be something as simple as this: To overcome mental suffering there is nothing more to do than to act insightfully in thought, word and deed in one's day to day life.

To understand the inner force of the Eightfold Path we must have a clear idea of the reason that compelled the Buddha to refer to it by the term "Middle Path". If we are not to bypass the intrinsic novelty of the Eightfold Path we must have a clear understanding of that reason. The term "Middle Path" as used in our contemporary everyday language is a harmless expression which nobody will object to. If a narrow road is bordered with deep drains on either side, no traveler on it will object to the advice asking him to avoid the extremes and take the middle path.

---

[1] MN. 1, 424, sutta 62

The Eightfold Path

But the Buddha presented his version of the Middle Path to a group of five ascetics whom he knew very well. He had lived with them for nearly six years and experimented with their form of religious life. They were a group for whom sanctity consisted of regular fasts, religious penances, and as much aloofness from society as possible. While in their company he had followed their philosophy ungrudgingly and with great zeal.

Quite naturally he judged such a philosophy incompatible with his religious aspirations and of no avail to his goals in life. He parted company with these fellow ascetics but now, after his experience of religious enlightenment, it was to them he returned to propound his own newly developed philosophy. What he had to present was a non-ascetical and even an anti-ascetical philosophy. It was this philosophy that he introduced as a Middle path that avoided the two extremes of sensuality and asceticism.

With regard to the first extreme, what the Buddha says is nothing unusual. There is nothing new in the idea that a religious person should avoid a life of sensuality. No laborious arguments are necessary to prove the unsuitability of such an extreme as a religious path. No one and least of all, his ascetical audience would have challenged that. But his objection to asceticism as a way of religion is very different. Asceticism has from time immemorial been a tradition - sanctioned, society-approved way to religious liberation. The popular belief even today is that greater asceticism implies greater holiness.

The challenge of the philosophy of the Buddha is exactly there. He regards asceticism as something extrinsic to the purpose of religion and so, left no place for it in the Eightfold Path. He included in the Eightfold Path only activities that purified a mind and rightly oriented it. The revolution in religious ideas that he initiated thereby is not a small one.

Of course one could ask why the Buddha, who so firmly rejected asceticism, advocated a form of monasticism. The answer is simple. First of all, monasticism is not asceticism. Monasticism is only a form separation from family life and not necessarily a life of self-torture. Secondly, even though he was a monk and founder of a monastic order, he did not restrict his discipleship to monks. Lay persons too were among his full-fledged disciples. But what is still more important for us to note is that the type of monasticism he advocated was the most liberal and the least ascetical of all the monastic systems that history had known until then.

It is unfortunate however, that contemporary Buddhist monasticism does not represent adequately the philosophy of the Middle Path in its original form. Buddhism today (like all the religions of modern times for that matter) attaches an undue importance to the externals of religion.

For the Buddha, religion, as well as monasticism, was something primarily of the mind. This is probably best illustrated in his attitude towards the attire of monks. The latitude he gave his monks in the choice of garb will appear particularly to traditionalists, astounding. Today monks are distinguished from lay persons by the saffron robe they wear. In the days of the Buddha, most non-Buddhist ascetics also wore saffron colored robes. But from many early Buddhist texts, Buddha was indifferent to the dress of his monks. Contrary to tradition, he clearly approved the use of even lay garments, leaving to the individual monk the option of wearing religious habit or lay clothing.

He was indifferent to his own dress and there are clear indications that at times he wore lay garments. According to the Vinaya Pitaka on one occasion, when a devoted benefactor offered him a silk garment meant for the lay person, he accepted it and announced to the monks:

I allow you, monks, use of lay garments. He who wishes may use monastic garments. He who wishes may use lay garments. But with either, what I commend is the spirit of contentment.[2]

In later Theravada commentaries and particularly the "Samantha-pasadika", the chief commentary on the Vinaya composed seven to eight centuries later, this permission was construed to suit the rigorous practices prevailing at the time. "Lay garments" were interpreted as garments given by lay persons with the expectation that they would be dyed saffron before being worn. But such a false explanation does not do justice to either the Buddha's Middle Path Philosophy or to the original scriptural texts.

The anti-ascetical attitude of the Buddha, of which this latitude regarding the monastic garb is one example, is not the only thing that is revolutionary in the philosophy of the Middle Path. There are many other revolutionary elements contained in it. His disregard for rites

---

[2] VP. MG, 280, viii, 1:35

The Eightfold Path

and ritual as also for the worship of gods and goddesses are two others.

Thus from numerous angles it is very clear that his Middle Path religion, of which the sole purpose was the healing of sick minds, is more revolutionary than would appear at first sight. The essence of religion for the Buddha and which he summed up in his sermon on the Four Noble Truths is very simple but very challenging. According to him, suffering is caused by a disoriented mind seeking fulfillment of immature emotional desires. Liberation is achieved by a rightly oriented mind practicing the Eightfold Path or more briefly the four characteristics of human nobility, loving kindness (mettā), compassion (karunā), gentleness (mudhitā) and equanimity (upekkhā). The mind of a liberated person is in a permanent state of peace. That peace is indestructible even by bodily death.

World Religions
Part Three
Christianity (with Judaism)

Chapter 1
Christianity Today and Christianity at the Beginning

It is difficult to describe what Christianity is today, because it is difficult to find out who Christians are. Christians never use the name "Christian" to introduce themselves. If any of them is asked what his or her religion is the answer received will be one such as: "I am a Catholic", "I am an Anglican, a Baptist, a Methodist, a Jehovah's Witness, a Pentecostal, a Member of the Assembly of God, a Mormon". This is because Christianity today is divided into a large number of denominations.

1. Divisions in Contemporary Christianity

What is stranger still is that a member of one denomination does not know anything about other denominations except that they are all illegitimate and false. Members of any denomination consider only their organization as true and authentic.

The fragmentary nature of religion is not specific to Christianity. There is not a single religion, whether Hinduism, Buddhism, Judaism or Islam, that has just one form. But this fragmentariness has affected Christianity more drastically than any other religion. According to the "World Christian Encyclopedia" produced by David Barret in 1982,[1] there were then over 20,780 independent Church denominations. Today several decades after the book's publication, that number could well be double. With such a diversity of forms, not just outsiders but even Christians would be at a loss to find out what Christianity is.

This was of course not so in the early days of Christianity. In early Christianity which focused attention on educating individuals to live their life under the guidance of the Divine Spirit or their enlightened conscience, conversion was by conviction. But the situation changed three centuries after the life of Jesus when an emperor of the Roman Empire converted to Christianity and declared Christianity as a religion approved within the Roman Empire.

Until then it was a forbidden religion in the Empire. Not long after it became an approved religion Christianity became a politically institutionalized religion. The Christian community became identical

---

[1] Barett David B, World Christian Encyclopedia A Comparative study of Churches and Religions in the Modern World AD 1900-2000 (Oxford University Press 1982) p.3

with the Empire community at the beginning and eventually with national communities. Governors of nations wielded greater power than Church leaders. Often each country or section of a country had its own version of Christianity.

Powerful Christian nations conquered powerless nations diffusing thereafter their own version of Christianity. Conversion by conviction changed to conversion by conquest. How Christianity a religion originally committed to the spiritual liberation of individuals became politicized is difficult to understand or explain.

Possibly that is the way in which religion and society are destined to evolve as the world becomes multitudinous. Happily however there are large numbers of thinking Christians in all denominations who still adhere to the concept of spiritual liberation.

50. 2. Forms of Church Today

To facilitate recognizing the diverse forms of Christianity along with their origin, historians have evolved a scheme that includes all the denominations under four umbrella groups. The groups are:
1) Roman Catholic Church
2) Eastern Orthodox Churches
3) Protestant Churches
4) New or Post-Protestant Churches

Even though the division does not reveal much, at least it helps us to get a rough idea of the historical evolution of Christianity. Soon after Christianity became a politically institutionalized religion, it began to get divided into parts. Christians of the Western part of the Empire, of which Rome was the capital, came to be called the "Roman Catholic Church" and this Church adhered to the form of culture of the region keeping Latin as its main language. It had one head called the "Pope" who was also considered "infallible" in matters of ecclesiastical administration.

Members of the Eastern part of the empire belonged to provincially distinct groups called "Orthodox Churches". Each provincial Church had its own head called the Patriarch. The union of Orthodox Churches retained its Middle Eastern form of culture with Constantinople as its capital and Greek as its main language.

The third group of churches called in common "Protestant Churches" consisted of Christian groups which broke away from the Roman Catholic Church and the headship of the Pope in the fifteenth century. The first party to break away was the one lead by a German monk called Martin Luther who disagreed with the Pope on a doctrinal matter. That group paved the way to a number of sub-groups.

The second party was headed by King Henry the 8th of England. He broke away from the pope over a political matter. The Church established by him in England was called the "Anglican Church", but that too initiated a number of branch-churches.

The fourth section called "New or Post-protestant Churches" is more difficult to decipher and describe. They are of very recent origin. They started to develop only from the latter part of the eighteenth century. Their number is so great that they are almost uncountable. Some of them are socially and religiously very active and are now spread out in many countries. Because of the techniques they employ to pacify depressed minds and because of the economic assistance they give to needy members, some of those churches are very popular.

Of the four groups of Churches the first three, namely, the Roman Catholic, the Orthodox and the Protestant are generally referred to as "Mainline Churches". This may be due to the fact that in matters of beliefs, rites and administration they have a number of aspects in common. But the more important reason could be that the members of those three Church bodies want to keep themselves apart from the large number of independent denominations of much later origin.

There is no doubt that many will get intrigued by the way Christianity has evolved into such a large number of divisions and subdivisions. Of the divisions themselves, all that we can say is that in a religion as widespread, and as long-lasting as Christianity they are inevitable. Denominations could even be useful as long as there are no conflicts and only good relationship between them. Conflicts of course cannot be avoidable when a denomination is linked to a political power and is controlled by it.

In a brief study of Christianity such as this we need not go more into detail about the multiple versions of Christianity. But keeping in mind the fragmentation of Christianity is indispensable for an impartial understanding as also evaluation of Christianity.[2]

---

[2] For more information see, Antony Fernando, Christian Path to Mental Maturity, (Intercultural Book Promoters, 4th ed.) p.107-119

51. 3. Link of Christianity with Judaism

A second fact of equally great importance for an objective understanding of Christianity is its relationship to Judaism. The divided state of Christianity briefly described above is indispensable for anybody to grasp what Christianity is today. But nobody will be able to grasp what Christianity was at the beginning and how it originated without some idea of its relationship with Judaism.

As a rule, no religion of today can be properly understood without taking into account the religions that existed in the same area prior to it. But probably no religion is so closely dependent on another as Christianity is on Judaism. Christianity actually grew out of it. Judaism is what gave birth to Christianity. Jesus, Christianity's founder, was born and died a Jew. He never abandoned Judaism nor did he dissociate himself from it. In the ministry, his primary concern was to correct the wrong ways in which his people practiced Judaism.

Christians of today do not talk much of their Jewish roots. When explaining their history, they do not, as a rule, go beyond the life-time of their founder. That is because they want to ensure the distinctness of their institutional identity. To begin the history of Christianity from Jesus would be as incorrect as to begin the history of Protestantism from Luther. Protestantism is a reform of Christianity as Christianity is of Judaism. Christianity cannot be understood without taking into account Pre-Christian Judaism.

The inner affinity between the two is well established by the fact that the Scriptures of the Jewish religion are an integral part of the Christian Scriptures. Christians have taken over the Jewish Scriptures exactly as they are without making any alteration in them.

The Jewish Scriptures are commonly referred to today as the "Hebrew Bible". The word "Hebrew" points to the language in which they were first written. "Bible" comes from the Greek for "book". At the stage when the Bible consisted of just the five books of Law, it was referred to as the "Law" and when the writings of the prophets were added to it as the "Law and the Prophets". The Jews looked at their Bible as the book par excellence. Keeping to the practice of the time, Jesus referred to it either as "the Law" or "the Law and the Prophets". He conformed to what was stated in it. He did not want to change anything in the Hebrew Bible.

Do not suppose that I have come to abolish the Law and the Prophets; I did not come to abolish, but to complete. I tell you this: so long as heaven and earth endure, not a letter, not a stroke, will disappear from the Law until all that must happen has happened.[3]

The Christian Scriptures however are not restricted to the Hebrew Bible. Christians have a collection of their own writings too. These contain information about the life and activities of Jesus as well as about the community of the first Christians. The two parts, the Jewish and the Christian, are today commonly treated as one book. In size the two parts are far from equal. The second is much smaller than the first. If we take a common size Bible such as the popular version of the "New English Bible"[4] the first or the Jewish part extends to as many as 1164 pages but the second or the exclusively Christian part has only 313 pages, which means that the first part is more than three times that of the second. The Christians name the Hebrew Bible, the "Old Testament" and their books the "New Testament".

In the religious language of the Jews (known in early times as Israelites) "testament" meant "covenant", "contract" or "bond". They believed that they were a race joined to God by a special bond. Such a claim is not exclusive to the Jews. Most ancient communities claimed that they had a special link with a god or goddess, and that this deity was their protector. In the way the Jews understood their testament, God had to protect the Israelite people and the Israelites had to observe the Law of God.

Accepting the same term, the Christians called the Hebrew Scriptures the "Old Testament" and their own writings the "New Testament". The word "old" here should not be taken as meaning "outdated" or "obsolete"; It only means that the Christians, while respecting the Jewish conviction that they, as one tribe of the world, had a special covenant with God, believed in another covenant – one more universal – that God had with the whole of humankind. That is what is underlined in the New Testament. From what has been said it is evident that a good grasp of the Hebrew Bible is important for the understanding of Christianity. In the form found today as also in Jesus" time, the Hebrew Bible consists of three parts, i) the Law, ii) the Prophets, and iii) the Writings. In our next chapter we will see them in summary form.

---

[3] Mt 5: 17-18

[4] Bible quotations in this book are taken from The New English Bible (Oxford University Press, Cambridge University Press 1970)

Chapter 2
Judaism the Mother-Religion of Christianity

To understand what Judaism is, we should have at least some idea of what the Jewish scriptures are, and very especially of what is at their basis namely, belief in an almighty God. This is also what is called monotheism. Judaism is most likely the oldest of the monotheistic religions in existence. Two other monotheistic religions today are Christianity and Islam, and they have both taken their concept of monotheism from Judaism.

Monotheism is far from being the basis of all religions. Hinduism has both polytheism and monotheism. But its monotheism is different from that of Judaism. Hindus consider the supreme divinity "Brahman" as an impersonal reality. Buddhism is neither polytheistic nor monotheistic. It leaves out completely the concept of God. The monotheism of Judaism is very special. To understand that specialty it has to be looked at from diverse angles. Four are outlined below.

(1) As any thinking person will understand, the notion of one almighty God is not a reality as such. Even though many traditional believers will be taken aback at that statement, there is no doubt that an almighty god is only a picture or mythical expression of a humanly incomprehensible supra-human reality. Moses, who according to the Bible book of Exodus is the creator of the Jewish form of monotheism, was aware that the reality referred to as God is incapable of being picturized. That is why in the very first of the Ten Commandments he forbade the Jewish people to make any carved image of God. The Ten Commandments were composed by Moses but shown in the Bible as delivered by God.

Nonetheless, he actually spoke of God using the image of a personal entity. That is because he knew that ordinary people felt compelled to follow laws, only if they were shown that there was a powerful law-giver and a judge above them. For any religion to be workable, and for any religious instruction, especially to children possible, the invisible mysterious reality has to be made imaginable. Talk of God as an almighty person is unavoidable and therefore fully justifiable.

(2) Another aspect of Moses" monotheism is that in its origin, it is more political than religious. Moses" first concern was not religion but race. He was primarily a lover of his tribal community. When he

saw that his people – the Israelites – were employed as slaves under the Pharaohs of Egypt he wanted to liberate them and transform them into an independent stable race with a land of their own. He was an astute statesman. Going against rigid opposition he rescued them from the control of the Pharaohs, and taking them in secret out of Egypt he settled them in the desert temporarily, looking forward to a day when a more fertile land could be found for their habitation. He was thus primarily a liberator of his own people like Mahatma Gandhi or Nelson Mandela in our times.

(3) But he felt that another requirement had to be fulfilled if his work of liberation was to be complete and permanent. This is where he comes in as a far-sighted religious visionary. He saw that if the Israelites were to be an unconquerable people, it was not sufficient for them to be given just food and drink and may be military training for self-protection. They had also to be mentally and spiritually strengthened. Every single Jew had to be endowed with a strong and righteous character. In other words, his people had to be trained to follow right life-values.

To get them to follow right life-values he evolved a novel strategy. He told the Jews that they were a race specially chosen by God and destined to live in close union with him. He said that this union was sealed by a contract or testament that God had made known to him. According to that testament the Jewish people had to follow God's commands, and if they did so, God was bound to protect them till the end of time. It is through this chosen-race idea that he got the Jews to accept that real religion was not a matter of worship but a matter of right conduct. Moses was thus an astute politician as an insightful character builder.

(4) A final point to take note of is how Jewish monotheism differs from that of Christianity as also of Islam. There is not the least doubt that the life-values upheld by the Jewish form of monotheism are valid not just for the Jews. Those life-values have power to bring spiritual liberation to people of any race or nation. If Christianity and Islam adopted the Jewish form of monotheism it was because they were aware of the universal applicability of its life-values.

But what is extra-ordinary about Judaism is that its monotheism was restricted to just the Jewish community. This is because Moses" sole concern was the welfare of the Jews. He wanted them to be a politically stable self-governing race in the world. Strictly speaking Judaism is not a missionary religion. They may wage wars to defend themselves and protect their habitation but never to spread their monotheism outside their region.

In this regard, Christians are different. Three centuries after the life of their Founder, Christianity became a religion that could invade other nations with the aim of establishing what was termed the Kingdom of God. In Islam, the diffusion of religion through political conquest started already from the life time of the Founder.

The only other religion of the type of Judaism is Hinduism. Jews restricted themselves to a race, Hindus to a land. Hindus too are not likely to invade another land to diffuse Hinduism. Hinduism and Judaism could be considered the two oldest religions of our times. In comparison with Hinduism, Judaism, of course, is a very small religion. According to statistics in 1992, there were only 15 million Jews.

We will now examine in brief the Jewish scriptures to see how its monotheism gave the Jewish people a special vision of life and taught them the values they had to put into practice. We will restrict ourselves to just four aspects of the vision of life brought out by the Jewish form of monotheism.

52. 1. Belief in One Life-giving God
53. 2. Example of Abraham, Father of Monotheism

According to the Jewish version of monotheism, life in its concrete individualized form is not a reality that develops by itself or survives on its own resources. Human beings are enlivened mysteriously. If they put their trust in that creative power, they get the means necessary to solve their problems and overcome adversities.

A proof of that dimension of God-belief is Abraham, whom the Jews consider not only as the father of their race, but also as the model God-believer. Abraham was a chieftain who lived in Ur of Mesopotamia. He was relatively well off, but there was one desire in his life that remained unfulfilled. He and his wife had no children. At the time that the Bible starts speaking of him, he was too old to have a child. He was one hundred years old. He discusses his problem with God. He is skeptical and so asks God how his dream could ever be realized.

"Can a son be born to a man who is a hundred years old? Can Sarah bear a son when she is ninety?"[1]

The story is a lesson on the power that protects human life. It is Abraham's faith in life's miraculous power of protection that is shown here symbolically as belief in a personal God. In spite of his initial skepticism, Abraham believes in God, and his faith is rewarded. He is blessed with a child.[2] The story points to the fact that the Life-Power of the universe is always by the side of human beings to offer them assistance. This Life-Power, whether we call it Universe, Nature, God or Life, is concerned with the individual needs of all human beings, whether this be food, shelter, progeny or liberation from any agony. But for that Power to become effective, the life-bearer must put his or her full trust in it.

The lesson taught by the second part of the story is still more illuminative. It shows what it is to place one's faith or trust in God. According to that part of the story Abraham was asked by God to sacrifice to him Isaac his only son. That request may sound uncanny to a modern person but there have been times when not only animals but also human beings were sacrificed to gods.

Isaac was the only child Abraham possessed, his only source of security for his future. Without Isaac his future as well as his entire life would be empty. But Abraham had a greater faith in life and its values than in his own progeny. He readily obeyed. He prepared the fire for the sacrifice. When God saw the selfless spirit of Abraham, he was satisfied. He stopped the sacrifice and provided through an angel, a ram for the purpose.

From time immemorial sacrifice of living beings has been taken as a sublime expression of the worship of God. This is because it is a symbol of a person's submission to right values of life as opposed to subservience to selfish desires. The self tries to find security through possessions. But could a human being possess anything? As the Buddha says in the Dhammapada (ch.5 verse 3), "If one does not possess one's own life, how can one possess one's own sons and daughters?" Faith in the one and only God therefore, is nothing other than a deep and selfless trust in the real values of life as opposed to those that are self-centered and therefore illusory. Taken in that sense the above mentioned story of Abraham is the best and the most authentic illustration of what genuine belief in one God implies.

---

[1] Gen 17:17
[2] Gen 21:1

54. 3. Living in Harmony with the Universe

The second great insight of the Jewish people regarding life was about the relationship of human beings to the cosmos. As they saw it, human beings were part of a great universe with its sun, moon, stars, trees and animals. The universe was their home. It was something to be loved and cherished.

The fact that they are an integral part of the universe should not be taken for granted. They must learn to safeguard the relationship. The story of Creation given in the very first page of the Bible was meant to give people the instruction they required in that regard.

In the beginning of creation, when God made heaven and earth, the earth was without form and void, with darkness over the face of the abyss, and the spirit of God was hovering over the surface of the waters. God said, "Let there be light", and there was light; so evening came, and morning came, the first day. God said, "Let the waters under heaven be gathered into one place, so that dry land may appear," and so it was. God called the dry land earth, and the gathering of the waters he called seas; and God saw that it was good...

God said "Let the earth bring forth living creatures, according to their kind: cattle, reptiles, and wild animals, all according to their kind"...and he saw that it was good...Then God said, "Let us make man in our image and likeness to rule the fish in the sea, the birds of heaven, the cattle, all wild animals on earth, and all reptiles that crawl upon the earth."

So God created man in his own image; ... male and female he created them. God blessed them and said to them "Be fruitful and increase, fill the earth and subdue it, rule over the fish in the sea, the birds of heaven, and every living thing that moves upon the earth... God saw all that he had made, and it was very good. Evening came, and morning came, a sixth day

On the sixth day God completed all the work he had been doing, and on the seventh day he ceased from all his work.[3]

The Old Testament story shows us how the Jewish tradition looked at life and the universe. For them the universe was one united whole. There is more unity to the universe than we can imagine. When taken as a whole, the universe is one body animated, as it were, by one living soul. The very Spirit or the Breath of God is in it.

---

[3] Gen 1:1 - 2:3

According to the story, the universe began when "the Spirit of God was hovering over the surface of the waters".

As the Jews saw it, human beings are endowed with a responsibility in the management of the world in so far as they were images of God, the master-planner and master-maker. Human beings are not the makers of the universe, but they are its careful maintainers and its developers. They have to care for the world, and make it "fruitful".

The creation story has a lesson for a better understanding of society too. God created the whole of mankind and not just the Jews (or the Christians). Human beings of any shape, color, culture or religion, are the product of God. When we take all these aspects together, we have to say that the belief of the Jews in God the creator is the outcome of the very positive way in which they looked at life, mankind and the universe.

Strictly speaking, the creation story has nothing to do with the historical origins of the universe. The teaching in it is not addressed to paleontologists, or people researching into the origins of life. It is a meditation meant to make people recognize their creature-liness as also their inner nobility. It awakens people to the importance of loving the universe and living in constant communion with it. In life and in death human beings are part of the universe which is animated by the Spirit of God.

Nothing shows people the invisible face of God as the visible mystery of the universe. In short, the Creation narrative is a pointer to the attitudes of joy, admiration, gratitude, hope, and responsibility with which human beings should embellish their life on earth.

55. 4. Reason for Failure of Marriages

Judaism has a great lesson to teach human beings on how they should spend their lives in the two distinct forms of man and woman. This is taught through the story of the creation of the first man called Adam and the first woman called Eve. That no doubt, is a concocted story because a demonic serpent is one of its main characters. But its message is very valuable. On one side, it shows what a sublime state of life marriage is. On the other, it shows the reason for the failure of most current marriages.

The story begins by saying that God needed a gardener to maintain his land and that he produced a man for that task by taking a handful of dust from the ground and breathing his life into it. If that is how God made man, then it is clear that every human being consists of two parts, a part that is mortal because it consists of a perishable body, and a part that is immortal, because God's breath is within him. After creating the man God gave him an unusual command to follow.

"You may eat from every tree in the garden, but not from the tree of the knowledge of good and evil; for on the day that you eat from it, you will certainly die".[4]

What the order seems to mean it this: Even from fruit seek pleasure in a law-abiding way and not in a greed-fulfilling way. Soon after handing over the garden to Adam, God saw the need of a companion for him. When producing the woman, He saw to it that the man and the woman were intrinsically linked.

And so he put the man into a trance and while he slept he took one of his ribs and closed the flesh over the place. The Lord God then built up the rib which he had taken out of the man into a woman...... (Gen.2:21-22)

It was thus that God established the state of marriage and family life to keep the world populated with human beings till the end of time. To achieve that purpose, men and women have to couple themselves together and jointly engage in the task of procreating progeny. To make procreation easy and pleasant to perform, God took steps to provide the man and the woman with distinct shapes that were enticing to each other and also to make all physical dealings between them pleasurable to each other.

But according to the story, God could not achieve the plan he desired. Adam and Eve chose to discard the order of God and yielded to the temptation proposed to them by the demonic serpent. The form of the temptation is clear from the answer given by the serpent when Eve explained to it God's warning that they would die if they ate the forbidden fruit.

Of course, you will not die. God knows that as you eat it, your eyes will be opened and you will be like gods knowing both good and evil. When the woman saw that the fruit of the tree was good to eat, and that it was pleasing to the eye and tempting to contemplate she took some and ate it. She also gave her husband some and he ate it. Then the eyes of both of them were opened and they discovered that they were naked. (Gen. 4:4-7)

---

[4] Gen 2: 15-17

Such a temptation was possible only because the faculty called the mind that human beings are endowed with can operate at one of two levels, at an immature pleasure-seeking level or at an enlightened law-abiding level. For the immature person, right is what pleases him and wrong what displeases him. In male-female dealings, an immature person is bent on seeking pleasure exclusively for pleasure's sake whereas an enlightened person seeks pleasure exclusively for the fulfillment of the purpose for which the pleasure is intended. In fact, it is such mental immaturity within each individual that is generally symbolized as the demonic tempter.

This story of temptation has much to do with what Gautama the Buddha taught in his sermon of the Four Noble Truths. According to the Buddha all human beings are born to suffer. But suffering is not insurmountable. This is because suffering arises from a pleasure-thirsty disoriented mind; and it is done away with by a duty-fulfilling enlightened mind.

Adam and Eve were mentally immature and so they failed to be law-abiding and got driven out of the Garden of Eden to live their life in pain and sorrow. Their behavior unfortunately has become the model that most married couples who are mentally immature follow today. It is for that reason that most people today fall into the pathetic situation of having to live their marital life in pain and misery. But according to the story there is also a way for anybody to make his or her married life happy and peaceful. It is to become law-abiding and keep united in heart with the Supreme Being who gave them their life.

56. 5. Basic Obligations of a Human Being

A fourth Jewish insight which is of benefit to people of any caste or creed is the one into the obligations that individuals have to fulfill to acquire humanness of the perfect form. The Jews looked at such obligations as imposed by God and so referred to them as "Commandments of God" or as the "Law of God".

To make it easy for ordinary people to remember those obligations, they were summed up in a formula that we today refer to as the "Ten Commandments". It is given in two books of the Pentateuch, namely Exodus [5] and Deuteronomy [6]. The one in the

---

[5] Ex 20: 1-21
[6] Deut 5: 6-21

Exodus is as follows. (N.B. The numbers indicating the commandments are added.)

God spoke and these were his words:

I am the Lord your God who brought you out of Egypt, out of the land of slavery.

1) You shall have no other God to set against me.

You shall not make a carved image for yourself nor the likeness of anything in the heavens above, or on the earth below, or in the waters under the earth. You shall not bow down to them or worship them; for I, the Lord your God, am a jealous god. I punish the children for the sins of the fathers to the third and fourth generations of those who hate me. But I keep faith with thousands, with those who love me and keep my commandments.

2) You shall not make wrong use of the name of the Lord your God; The Lord will not leave unpunished the man who misuses his name.

3) Remember to keep the Sabbath day holy.

You have six days to labor and do all your work. But the seventh day is the Sabbath of the Lord your God; that day you shall not do any work, you, your son or your daughter, your slave or your slave girl, your cattle or the alien within your gates; for in six days the lord made heaven and earth, the sea and all that is in them, and on the seventh day he rested. Therefore the Lord blessed the Sabbath day and declared it holy.

4) Honor your father and mother that you may live long in the land which the Lord your God is giving you.

5) You shall not commit murder.

6) You shall not commit adultery.

7) You shall not steal.

8) You shall not give false evidence against your neighbor.

9-10) You shall not covet your neighbor's house; you shall not covet your neighbor's wife, his slave, his slave-girl, his ox, his ass, or anything that belongs to him.

When all the people saw how it thundered and the lightening flashed, when they heard the trumpet sound and saw the mountain smoking, they trembled and stood at a distance. "Speak to us yourself" they said to Moses "and we will listen; but if God speaks to us we shall die". Moses answered, "Do not be afraid. God has come only to test you, so that the fear of him may remain with you and keep you from sin." So the people stood at a distance, while Moses approached the dark cloud where God was.

As given in the Bible, the Ten Commandments formed the basis of the civic constitution of the Jewish people; but the respect for right values shown here as a vital requirement for the survival and stability of the Jewish community, is of equal validity to people of any other. People of any race or country have to uphold those principles if they are to achieve the progress and prosperity of their community.

The first two Commandments outline the sense of religion that individuals should be guided by if they are to achieve fulfillment in their personal life. What the two commandments say is that, if people want to be truly human, truly noble, truly divine, they must seek goodness and right values with all their heart, with all their soul, with all their strength, with all their mind.

The third Commandment too, though addressed to just the Jewish community, contains a lesson of universal value. The obligation of taking a day's rest every week reminds people that just as no-work makes a person a beggar, over-work can make him a wreck. Work without due rest can be motivated by avarice and could lead to ill-health.

Of the Ten Commandments, the last seven form a unified whole and show the responsibilities that members of a community have to fulfill in their dealings with each other. Of these the 4th (Honor thy father and mother) the 6th (You shall not commit adultery) and the 10th (You shall not covet another's wife) are meant to safeguard the most basic unit of the human society, the family.

The remaining four namely the 5th (You shall not kill), the 7th with the 9th (You shall not steal the goods of others or even covet them) and the 8th (You shall not bear false witness) show that human beings have responsibilities not just to their own family but also to the entire community. The members of a community cannot hurt others, deceive others or exploit others. They should abstain from destroying not just the life of individuals, but even their character or their future.

What the Ten Commandments say of the family or social responsibilities of individuals has its parallels in other cultures and other religions. The "Five Moral Precepts" (Pancha Seela) of religions which belong to the Indian tradition such as Hinduism and Buddhism express the same though in the form of "vows": 1) I vow to abstain from taking life. 2) I vow not to misappropriate the possessions of others. 3) I vow to abstain from indulging in wrong sexual behavior.

4) I vow to abstain from telling lies. 5) I vow to abstain from taking intoxicants. The Jewish "Commandments" and the Indian "Precepts" have much in common.

If we have analyzed somewhat lengthily the notion of God-belief in the Old Testament, it is primarily because Christianity cannot be understood without a right grasp of the Jewish idea of God-belief. Jesus himself did nothing more than clarify to his listeners the notion of God-belief in the Jewish Bible.

Chapter 3
The New Testament Miracle Stores in the Gospels

The Bible of the Christians includes, as mentioned earlier, not only the Hebrew Scriptures but also a collection of their own writings. This collection called the New Testament is what one must examine to learn about Christianity in its earliest and most authentic form.

In the form recognized by Christians of all denominations, the New Testament consists of 27 separate books or writings. The writings are so small that it is better to call them booklets than books. The biggest among them is only about thirty pages while there are some that are not more than two or three pages each. Taking into account their content, their aims, and their writing styles, the books are traditionally divided into four groups:

a) Gospels (four books in all)
b) Acts of the Apostles (one book)
c) Epistles (21 in all)
d) Revelation (one book)

Since the books of the New Testament were written by different individuals and also to fit into situations that were not identical, the link and the cohesiveness of their content cause problems to readers of the Bible. That problem however gets easily solved if we keep in mind that all the books are woven around two principal themes. One is the life and ministry of Jesus, treated mainly in the Gospels. The other is the birth of the multi-racial Church dealt with in the other books of the New Testament. Once those two themes are kept in mind, connecting the content of the diverse books becomes relatively easy.

In this chapter we will examine just the first of the four groups namely the Gospels, paying special attention to one element in them that modern readers have difficulties with, namely, the miracle-stories.

57. Gospels

The best known among the books of the New Testament, and so also placed at the head, are the four Gospels. They are distinguished by the names of the authors they are traditionally attributed to. They are thus referred to as Gospel of Matthew, Gospel of Mark, Gospel of

Luke, and Gospel of John. The word "Gospel" means in Greek "good news" or more tangibly, "news of relief from pain and suffering". Jesus used the word "Gospel" at the very inauguration of his ministry.

After John had been arrested Jesus came into Galilee proclaiming the Gospel of God: "The time has come, the kingdom of God is upon you; repent and believe in the Gospel".[1]

The followers of Jesus saw not only his message but the preacher himself as a source of great relief and so a "good news". Because of that they called the very life-accounts of Jesus "Gospels".

Of the four Gospels, the first three, namely, Matthew, Mark and Luke have in both writing style and content many common points or parallels. Because of this similarity, these three Gospels are referred to by Bible analysts as the "Synoptic Gospels". "Synoptic" means "seen from one view".

The fourth Gospel, the one by John, is of later origin and of an altogether different style. It is more a meditative study of the significance of Jesus for the reawakening of mankind in general. Its message is expressed with great dependence on poetic symbols. The Gospel of John is considered to be also a study of Christian spirituality and mysticism presented within the framework of a life of Jesus.

In their literary form however, all the four Gospels are basically religious biographies of Jesus. Though they contain many historical details, they are primarily intended by their authors to be "life-stories" of Jesus rather than "life-histories". The Gospels did not originate as historical records but as books of religious instruction. They were built up on sermons and meditational reflections that the early Church leaders presented at the religious assemblies of Christians or in classes meant for converts to Christianity.

58. Miracle-stories

Jesus is presented in all the four Gospels primarily as a healer. He healed people by his miracles. And to heal people it looks as if he did one miracle after another. The miracle is given such a prominent place in the Gospels that they could easily appear as books of miracle-stories. The following text from the Gospel of Mark shows this.

---

[1] Mk 1:15

The New Testament

They (i.e. Jesus and his disciples) came to Capernaum and on the Sabbath he went to the synagogue and began to teach...Now there was a man in the synagogue possessed by an unclean spirit. He shrieked: "What do you want with us, Jesus of Nazareth, Have you come to destroy us? I know who you are, – the Holy One of God?" Jesus rebuked him: Be "silent...and come out of him". And the unclean spirit...with a loud cry left him.

On leaving the synagogue, they went straight to the house of Simon and Andrew... Simon's mother-in-law was ill in bed with fever. They told him about her at once. He came forward, took her by the hand, and helped her to her feet. The fever left her and she waited upon them.

That evening after sunset they brought to him all who were ill or possessed by devils; and the whole town was there gathered at the door. He healed many who suffered from various diseases, and drove out many devils. He would not let the devils speak, because they knew who he was....

Once he was approached by a leper, who knelt before him begging his help. "If only you will", said the man, "you can cleanse me". In warm indignation, Jesus stretched out his hand, touched him, and said, "Indeed I will, be clean again." The leprosy left him immediately and he was clean. [2]

In Mark's Gospel, out of a total of 666 verses, as many as 209 or 31% deal directly with miracles. If we leave out the passion-narrative which contains very little of the miraculous element, we see that as much as 41% of Mark talks about miracles. Miracles are not only a big but also a very important part of the Gospels. If the Gospels are better known than most other books of the New Testament, it is because of the miracle-stories in them. People like stories. They remember stories well. The more striking, the better they are remembered. And there couldn't be anywhere in the world more striking stories than miracles. But miracles have another side to them. Modern people are ill at ease with miracles. For them, miracles border on the legendary. For many, miracles are more an obstacle to the appreciation of the Gospel message than a help.

Miracles are not easy to understand. The only way to understand them rightly is to take them in the light of the role they played in the community of the first Christians. That was to show who Jesus had

---

[2] Mk 1:21-42

been and what exactly had been his mission within the Jewish community. But if we are to see that connection between the miracle-stories and the mission of Jesus, there are a number of basic points that we have to keep in mind.

59. Main Reason for Emphasis on Miraculous Healings

If miracles are given such a prominent place in the Gospels, there is a very special reason for doing so. The picture of Jesus as an astounding healer had, from the view of the first Christians, who were mainly Jews, a very special function to fulfill.

For several decades before the birth of Jesus, the Jewish people were ruled by the Romans and subjected to great oppression under them. Earlier they had suffered under other rulers. Due to the suffering they were undergoing under foreign rule, they consoled themselves by saying that a redeemer appointed by God would come to their rescue. The redeemer was called Messiah in Hebrew or Christ in Greek literally "the redeemer appointed by God". During the lifetime of Jesus as also for some time afterwards, the followers of Jesus were exclusively Jews. The Jewish followers of Jesus needed an answer to give the Jews who asked them why they were following Jesus. Their answer was that for them Jesus was the expected redeemer or Christ. To prove that, they had to show, that Jesus actually brought them relief from pain and suffering. The picture that the Prophets had given of the Christ too was of such a redeemer. The text Jesus cited from Isaiah[3] at the very first sermon he gave to the people in the synagogue makes that clear.

The spirit of the Lord is upon me because he has anointed me;
He has sent me to announce good news to the poor,
to proclaim release for prisoners
and recovery of sight for the blind;
to let the broken victims go free,
to proclaim the year of the Lord's favor.[4]

Isaiah uttered those words when he wanted to declare that a New Jerusalem without suffering was going to dawn soon. The use of that citation by Jesus at his very first sermon shows that Jesus looked

---

[3] Isaiah 61:1-2
[4] Lk 4:18-19

at himself as a person endowed by God with the mission to bring relief to suffering Jewish people.

The Jewish concept of redeemer had two sides to it. Some took him as one who, like David of a long time ago, would bring an end to foreign rule and establish self-government in a land of their own. Others took him as a liberator of ordinary people who were undergoing pain and suffering due largely to corruption and malpractices prevailing in society. Jesus looked at himself as a redeemer of the second sense.

Taken in that sense his view of liberation was close to that of the Buddha discussed earlier. The Buddha too wanted to heal people of their sufferings. His method too had nothing to do with politics. His method of curing people of suffering was changing their minds. According to him suffering ceased when a selfish mind changed into a selfless one.

Jesus himself did not rely on politics. He too wanted to redeem people from suffering by changing their minds. But he did so by using the method indicated in the Bible which is that of submission to right life-values through the strength given by the Divine Spirit. The main sufferers that Jesus took into consideration were those treated as outcasts of society such as publicans (tax-gatherers), Samaritans, lepers, sinners, prostitutes and individuals who, because of their behavioral disorders, were considered possessed by the devil.

He brought relief to them mainly by his compassionate acceptance of them as human beings equal to all others. He also imparted to them the mental strength they needed to become fully human. People, who acquired healing and mental peace through his teachings, accepted Jesus as their redeemer. They told the non-Christian Jews that they followed Jesus because he brought them relief from their inner suffering.

60. Jesus' Refusal to be a Wonder-worker

To understand miracles properly, we must distinguish them from wonders. Miracles uplift suffering people. They bring relief and liberation. But wonders only astonish and mystify. True saints and sages never want to astonish people. They do not want to be referred to as wonder-workers or miracle-workers. Only false saints and sages desire that.

Buddha saw clearly the danger of such pretensions to sanctity and so he not only forbade his disciples from attempting to do wonders, but also made the very claim to such powers a disqualification to membership in his monastic order. Jesus didn't believe in wonders either. He condemned those who asked him to do a miracle as a sign of his authority.

"When the doctors of the Law and the Pharisees asked him "Master, we should like you to show a sign", Jesus replied, "It is a wicked, godless generation that asks for a sign".[5]

We see the same attitude in the picturized story of the temptation in the desert; there too, Jesus clearly expressed his distaste for appearing before the world as a wonder-worker. He refused to accede to the Satanic request to turn stone into bread or to jump down from the pinnacle and come out uninjured.[6]

61. Miracles an Outcome of Faith

Another very vital point to be pondered on is the explanation that Jesus gives about the way miracles take effect and the insistence he made about the possibility of everybody to perform miracles. Anybody with faith, that is, with a positive trust in the protective power of life is capable of working miracles. This is clear from what he told his disciples.

I tell you this: if you have faith no bigger even than a mustard-seed, you will say to this mountain, "Move from here to there" and it will move. Nothing will prove impossible for you.[7]

According to Jesus, anybody who has faith gets a miraculous strength to overcome problems, however big and insurmountable they may appear to be. Faith here stands for a realistic vision of life. Faith is generally interpreted as belief in the power of an almighty God residing in heaven. But as explained earlier, an almighty God as a personal entity is not a reality but the picturization or symbolic expression of an incomprehensible mysterious reality. That mysterious reality could well be a constituent element of the human being in its supra-terrestrial eternal dimension.

---

[5] Mt 12:38
[6] Mt 4:1-11
[7] Mt 17:20

If that is so, the power to overcome obstacles may be within the human being himself. Anybody who has faith in that supernatural power within oneself can work miracles. This is clear from words such as these that he spoke to those who were healed: "Stand up, and go on your way; your faith has cured you"[8]; "Take heart my daughter, your faith has cured you".[9]

Furthermore, the faith on which healing power rests is not faith in Jesus as such. Jesus was no doubt a positive aid for the people to gather up their faith. But the faith that healed was faith in God or more intelligibly, faith in the protective power of life. When that faith was missing Jesus was totally incapacitated. In his own village town of Nazareth for example, Jesus could not work any miracles because people had no faith.

He could work no miracles there, except that he put his hands on a few sick people and healed them. And he was taken aback by their want of faith.[10]

Not only in Nazareth, but even in any other place, if Jesus did not work miracles, that would not negate the fact that he was a miraculous healer. The main miracle he did was to awaken people to the divine power hidden within them which could enable them to heal themselves.

This brief explanation about the miracle-stories indicates that when read with insight and an open mind, the Gospels are not fairy tales or pious legends. If presented in secular language, what they teach is that by just correcting their disoriented minds, human beings can overcome their problems and difficulties. The Jews who understood the teachings of Jesus in that light took him as their redeemer and became his followers.

---

[8] Lk 17:19
[9] Mt 9:22
[10] Mk 6:5; Mt 10:1

Chapter 4
Life and Teachings of Jesus

Jesus was by race and religion a Jew. He lived in Palestine which the Jews considered their homeland. When Jesus was born however, his land was a colony of the Roman Empire. The supreme authority was the emperor in Rome. Jesus is traditionally believed to have been born in 01 AD. Our calendar counts its years from that year.

62. Life of Jesus

Very little is known about the life that Jesus led before he started his ministry. His mother was called Mary and she was married to a carpenter named Joseph. A remark about Jesus made by the inhabitants of his village and reported in the Gospels of Matthew and Mark indicates that he belonged to a rather big family. Members of his village after listening to a sermon of his queried:

"Is he not the carpenter's son? Is not his mother called Mary, his brothers James, Joseph, Simon, and Judas? And are not all his sisters here with us?"[1]

Since he himself was referred to by people as "carpenter"[2] or "son of the carpenter"[3], it is likely that he himself engaged in the trade of a carpenter. As in any village, also in Nazareth, his family's village, carpentry was a valued trade, and the carpenter a respected person. He could be expected to have known his trade well. As a Jew he knew his Bible well and without any doubt he would have meditated on its message profusely.

Judging from the exuberance that we see in him later, it is however difficult to imagine that he would have been the ordinary type of family-supporting carpenter limiting himself to his trade, his home and even his religion. He is a person who would have had an out-going temperament which enabled him to take an active part in the community affairs of the village. He certainly had leadership qualities. He had the capacity to gather a crowd to listen to him. He had an appealing power of speech. He could win over individuals to follow him.

---

[1] Mt 13:55; Mk 6:3
[2] Mk 6:3
[3] Mt 13:55

63. Meeting the Baptist

It was when he was about thirty, the age at which a person is normally considered mature, that he set off on his ministry. The exact circumstances that impelled him to launch into preaching are not clear. But the decision had much to do with his meeting John the Baptist, the hermit who preached by the river Jordan in Judea.

In his preaching, John openly denounced the corruption prevailing in the society of his day. To all who came, he preached the necessity of repentance and stressed the need for changing their selfish life-styles. His message was simple: "Repent the Kingdom of Heaven is upon you"[4]. Those who decided to follow his teaching, he subjected to a ritual bath (in Greek "baptisma") in the river.

According to the Gospels Jesus too went to be baptized by him. Probably he too wanted to join the group of reformed Jews preparing for the coming kingdom. But John knew Jesus well. They were children of two cousin sisters. John was senior to Jesus only by six months [5]. As a grown-up John was aware of the sublime life that Jesus led, and so, refused at first to baptize him. On the pressure of Jesus however, he yielded. But according to the Gospel of Matthew, something extra-ordinary happened when he came out of the water.

After baptism Jesus came out of the water at once, and at that moment heaven opened; he saw the Spirit of God descending like a dove to alight upon him; and a voice from heaven was heard saying, "This is my Son, my Beloved, on whom my favor rests".[6]

The supra-terrestrial language in which the incident is recounted shows how episodes of the life of Jesus were narrated in the early Christian community. If that devotion-created mythical language could be understood realistically what the passage says is that Jesus was a person with an unusual vision of right life-values. Because of that John took the opportunity of Jesus" visit to show that he was more suited than himself to undertake the ministry that the Jewish society urgently needed. Neither John nor Jesus had the slightest intention of creating another religion outside Judaism. What both of them wanted to do was to bring about a spiritual revival within Judaism.

---

[4] Mt 3:2
[5] Lk 1:36
[6] Mt 3:13-17

64. Ministry

Jesus started his ministry not in the same region as John, namely Judea, but in his own province of Galilee. But the message he started with was identical: "Repent, for the Kingdom of Heaven is upon you".[7] Judging from the manner in which Jesus started his ministry, it is evident that the example of John had a great impact on the mind of Jesus. One teaching of John that Jesus totally agreed with was that true religion was very different from religion of the clan-centric form. Race and religion are not identical. Nobody ever became religious by simply belonging to a race or an institution. Religion was adherence to right life-values and not adherence to beliefs and practices particular to a racial tradition. John made it absolutely clear that Judaism as a vision of Life-values had nothing to do with Jewish-ness as membership in a race. This is why he said:

Do not presume to tell yourselves, "We have Abraham for our father." I tell you that God can make children for Abraham out of these stones here.[8]

Between Jesus and John however, there was one difference. Each chose a different path for the execution of their ministry. John selected that of rigorous asceticism; Jesus opted for compassionate service. He wanted to bring healing to society while living within it.

To make his reform campaign among the Jews effective, Jesus selected a number of disciples and trained them for the task. Those closest to him were called "apostles" and their number is given as twelve. The ministry of Jesus was greatly appreciated by people of all walks of life, especially the ordinary people.

65. Man of Prayer

Prayer was an integral part in the life of Jesus. "Prayer" which is a religious exercise followed in theistic religions, is not very different from what is called "meditation" commonly practiced in Asian religions like Hinduism and Buddhism. Both prayer and meditation are ways of opening one's heart to the invisible but eternal reality of life. According to Mark, during the period of his ministry, Jesus started his day with prayer.

---

[7] Mt 4:17
[8] Mt 3:9

Life and Teachings of Jesus

Very early next morning, he got up and went out. He went to a lonely spot and remained there in prayer.[9]

Often also after finishing some ministerial activity, he retired to prayer. Matthew describes what he did after his preaching to a crowd of five thousand whom he had also supplied with food.

Then he made the disciples embark and go on ahead to the other side; after doing that he went up the hill-side to pray alone.[10]

At moments of crisis, he found guidance and courage in prayer. At Gethsemane he prepared for his arrest by prayer.

Jesus then came with his disciples to a place called Gethsemane. He said to them, "Sit here, while I go there to pray".[11]

The apostles saw Jesus engaged in prayer so often that once they asked him to teach them to pray.

He was praying in a certain place and when he ceased, one of his disciples said to him, "Lord, teach us to pray."[12]

In answer to that request, Jesus gave them a text which is almost certainly based on the type of prayer he himself used. The text which is known today as the "Lord's Prayer" is divisible into two parts.

i) Our Father in heaven, thy name be hallowed; thy kingdom come, thy will be done on earth as in heaven.

ii) Give us today our daily bread. Forgive us the wrong we have done, as we have forgiven those who have wronged us. And do not bring us to the test, but save us from the evil one.[13]

The first part is a greeting to the invisible power to which the prayer is addressed. The use of the term "Our Father" shows with what intimacy Jesus looked at the supreme power that governs the "heaven" and the "earth". The expression "The Kingdom come, thy will be done on earth as in heaven" clarifies the meaning of the term "kingdom of God" which he considered his mission to establish. The "kingdom of God" is just the place where the will of God prevails and

---

[9] *The Oxford Bible Reader's Dictionary and Concordance* (Oxford University press) London) p. 4-45

[10] Mt 6:25-33
[11] Lk 15; 11-32
[12] Lk 16: 19-31
[13] Lk 10:29-37

the law of God is observed. There is no political connotation to his idea of the "kingdom".

The second half is a series of petitions of which two are particularly noteworthy. Both of them seem to be based on the assumption that the praying person is a sinner. Of these, the first is the plea "Forgive us the wrong we have done, as we have forgiven those who have wronged us". This plea shows what individuals have to do to remedy the failures they have fallen into in the past. They need to ask God for forgiveness which is a way of saying that they have to repent in heart for what they have done and accept to correct themselves. The plea includes an important but also difficult condition. Realizing that forgiveness is received to the extent that forgiveness is given, those, who undertake to pray, have to accept to forgive those who have harmed them. For Jesus the readiness to forgive enemies is an indispensable requirement of a genuine God-believer.

The second plea is: "Do not bring us to the test, but save us from the evil one." The plea shows what precautions one has to take to avoid falling into wrong doings in the future. The word "test" translated also as "temptation" refers to the seductive desires that arise in the minds of individuals and which, if not arrested in time, make any person fall into sin. In the text, seductive desires are referred to as the "evil one" often called also "Satan".

Both these please seem to insinuate that all those who undertake to pray should do so keeping one conviction in mind. Everybody almost by a deficiency of birth is a sinner. But by controlling one's mind and observing the law of God, which is the same as one's conscience, anybody can become a saint and a member of the kingdom of God.

Jesus was a saint and one who had acquired through prayer an intimate unity with the divine. It was because of the extra-ordinary spirituality of Jesus, that the Jews who listened to him felt compelled to accept him as their redeemer.

66. End of the Ministry

Jesus" work however, did not appeal to the religious leaders. They saw his ideas of reform as a threat to their racialist version of Judaism. They campaigned against him before the Roman authorities,

Life and Teachings of Jesus

and secured his condemnation to death. Jesus ended his life through a death on the cross, the Roman equivalent of our present gallows.

Jesus could have escaped death by simply appeasing the religious leaders. But he did not want to accede to their misinterpretation of the Kingdom of God. Going against the prophetic teachings of the Bible, they took the kingdom of God as an earthly kingdom that is politically stable and independent, or in other words, as a kingdom of the Jews.

For Jesus, the kingdom of God was different. To belong to Jesus" version of the kingdom, individuals had to be committed to truth and justice and live rightly according to their conscience. Those who belonged to that kingdom lived in union with God now as also after their earthly existence.

Jesus willingly accepted to die for the version of the Kingdom he upheld. He did not fear death. He knew that death killed the body but not the spirit. That is why he celebrated his death at the sacred meal of the Paschal festival the day before his death. When breaking the bread for sharing and lifting the cup of wine for drinking he referred to the bodily torture and the bloodshed he was soon to undergo. He told the apostles to use the meal of bread and wine to celebrate the occasion after his death.

Later the apostles understood that for Jesus" death was not an end or a passing away, but the start of a higher supra-earthly eternal life. This is what the followers of Jesus pictorially represented eventually through the powerful image of the resurrection.

The life of Jesus was very short. According to a calculation of modern scholars, Jesus was born in 05 BC and died on Friday the 7th April 30 AD, which would mean that he was 35 years, when he died. Granted the brevity of Jesus" ministry, one is led to wonder if Jesus could have achieved much. But the strange fact is that what he taught the Jewish people about the spiritual or the personality-building side of Jewish monotheism became the basis of a multi-racial religion that we today call Christianity.

67. What Jesus Taught

To find out what was really special in his ministry to the Jewish people, we have to examine the message that his teaching contained. Of the numerous teachings of Jesus, we select the three we could consider the most decisive. They are: (1) Faith in a Protector God, (2)

Faith in a Forgiving God and (3) Positive concern for the needs of other human beings.

i. Faith in a Protector God

If people of all races and regions have from time immemorial flocked to shrines and sacred places, it is for no other reason than to seek relief from the suffering they are undergoing. People usually turn to God, a god, goddess or mysterious power to seek help when they are in need. Search for supra-earthly help by suffering human beings could well be the factor that has given birth to religion in its multifarious forms.

Through his insight into human nature, Jesus clearly saw that most human beings, because of their inability to overcome day to day problems were thwarted by feelings of inner anxiety and despair. There are numerous situations that bring about a psychological breakdown in people. At these moments, they come to such a state of despair and depression that they say to themselves: "No, I cannot." "I am finished." "There is nothing more I can do." It was to redeem human beings from such a state of despair and depression that Jesus taught the doctrine of faith in a Protector God.

But he had something very special to say about the effective way to adopt to achieve divine protection. He said that relief was automatic and given even without asking to one who gives priority to right living. He told them therefore to set their minds first on the values of the Kingdom or of one's conscience.

Therefore I bid you, put away anxious thoughts about food and drink to keep you alive, or clothes to cover your body. Surely life is more than food, the body more than clothes. Look at the birds of the air; they do not sow and reap and store in barns, yet your heavenly Father feeds them. You are worth more than the birds! Set your mind on God's Kingdom and his justice before everything else, and all the rest will come to you as well.

Faith in a Protector God may look mythical to a rationalistic person but if the picture is correctly grasped, what it says is that, in the worst circumstances of life, human beings have no reason to be depressed. Whether from above or from one's deep inner self, help was available to any needy person with a positive attitude to life. One of the main aims of Jesus" ministry was to show that the best way to overcome worry-causing problems was to live dutifully respecting the dictates of one's conscience.

ii. Faith in a Forgiving God

To cure human beings of another equally demoralizing and dehumanizing mental sickness, Jesus spoke of God as a person who forgives sins. To understand the value of forgiveness, we must visualize the extensiveness of the psychological damage that guilt feelings cause in a person. Guilt is different from sin. Sin makes a person morally unclean. Guilt makes a person mentally sick. Jesus used the doctrine of divine forgiveness to prevent people from getting mentally sick.

Jesus' doctrine of forgiveness is enshrined in his parable referred to as that of the "Prodigal Son" but which, to be more meaningful, should be called the parable of the "Benevolent Father". According to that story, the youngest son in a family decided to break away from the father, take his share of the family inheritance and go off to a distant land in search of worldly thrills. Not long after his departure, he made a mess of his life and realized the folly of his decision. In the resultant state of utter helplessness, he decided to go back home.

One would have expected the father of such a break-away son to have disowned the son on his departure, and to have thrown him out on his return. But this father was different. From the day of the son's departure, he yearned for his return, and when he did return, he welcomed him back with open arms. The benevolent father in the story is the ever-benevolent God. Through the story, Jesus sought to console those ridden with guilt feelings, saying to them that God, the universal source of goodness and life, does not reject them for their misdoings, and so, there is no reason for self-rejection.

There are many today who consider forgiveness as an incentive to further sinning or as an act of inattention to the goodness of the virtuous. In the story of the Prodigal Son, that attitude is taken by the elder son whose intervention is described in the second half of the parable.

Modern psychologists who understand the inner lesson of the story attach increasing therapeutic value to Jesus' doctrine of forgiveness. According to them every immature person is a split personality. The emotional self and the intuitive self are irreconcilably torn apart. Forgiveness represents the state when the intuitive self assures the emotional self "You are accepted by me." The split caused in the personality by the sense of guilt is thereby healed.

In the parable, the father represents Nature. Nature tells the fallen person: I understand you even if society does not. Society is represented by the elder son. If Jesus spoke of God often, it was not so much to make people understand God better, but to make them understand their human nature, and particularly their weaknesses, better. This is evident from his teachings on both Providence and forgiveness. He spoke of both a providing God and a forgiving God purely to make human beings internally stronger and mentally more mature.

iii. Concern for Others

There is according to Jesus a third deficiency in human beings that prevents them from achieving a truly human stature. It is blindness to their inner oneness with other human beings. Human beings are by essence inter-related, and they cannot be fully human if they do not live and practice their inter-relatedness. Jesus used three beautiful parables to point that out. The first is the story of the rich man and Lazarus. [12]

The rich man lived a life of luxury. He draped himself in rich clothes. He ate and drank sumptuously. At the entrance to his gate was Lazarus, a beggar, sick and covered with sores. His only food was the crumbs of bread fallen from the rich man's table, and brought to him by his servants. The story ends with the picture of what happens to these two after their death. Lazarus is in heaven; the rich man is in hell.

The lesson that Jesus puts across through this story is a powerful one. There was nothing in the behavior of the rich man that, according to popular assessment, was reproachable and could justify his being condemned to eternal hell-fire. There was nothing immoral in his life. He did not kill, steal or commit adultery. He did not hurt the poor man at the gate. He did not kick him as he passed by or throw him out; and after all, what is wrong in a person enjoying a good life if blessed with a rich inheritance? But Jesus says the rich man was guilty. He was guilty even to the extent of meriting hell-fire. His only crime was that he did not look at the poor man at the gate as a human being.

Jesus' second story is equally powerful. It is the story of the Good Samaritan. There are three characters in the story, a Jewish priest, a Jewish Levite and a Samaritan. The first two characters are symbols of accepted religious piety. The third is an outcast considered by the Jews as religiously impure. All of them meet one after the other, a helpless person fallen by the wayside, a victim of brigands. The first two see him and pass by. Probably they were in a hurry to officiate at a religious ceremony. The despised Samaritan alone comes to the poor man's rescue. It was the Samaritan that Jesus pointed to as the truly religious person, or the only mentally mature person in the group.

What the Samaritan was to the Jew of 2000 years ago, a Hindu or Buddhist would be to the Christian of today. In a parallel way, the Jewish priest and the Levite would be close to a Christian bishop and priest. Thus if broadly adapted to the twentieth century religious context what Jesus says is that the charitable Hindu or Buddhist is more religious than a self-conceited bishop or priest of the mechanically Christian type. For Jesus, it is only a person who is genuinely concerned with others that is truly religious.

The third parable is the one called the "Last Judgment". According to Jewish belief people were selected to the "Kingdom of God" after the Last Judgment.

The Kingdom of God was a concept that everybody in the Jewish community was well acquainted with. The majority of them, however, looked at it rightly or wrongly as something to come about at the "end of the world". Jesus too often made use of that popular end-of-the-world image when speaking of it but what he was really concerned with was its realization here and now. For him thus the Kingdom stood for a society of people doing the will of God on earth. Originally that is what the word "Church" stood for.

It is not our intention here to question the form that the Church has taken in the course of its long history. But we have to admit that what Jesus taught the Jews through the parable of the Last Judgment is equally applicable to members of the Church (or Churches) of today who call themselves Christians. In their own end-of-the-world language what Jesus told the Jews is as follows.

When the Son of Man comes in his glory... he will separate men into two groups, as a shepherd separates the sheep from the goats, and he will place the sheep on his right hand and the goats on his left.

Then the king will say to those on his right hand "You have my Father's blessing; come, enter and possess the kingdom that has been ready for you since the world was made. For when I was hungry you gave me food; when thirsty you gave me drink; when I was a stranger you took me to your home; when naked you clothed me; when I was ill you came to my help, when in prison you visited me".

Then the righteous will reply, "Lord, when was it that we saw you hungry and fed you, ... And the king will answer "I tell you this: anything you did for one of my brothers here, however humble, you did it for me.[14]

Though God is generally spoken of as an invisible reality according to this statement, there is one shape in which he is physically visible. That is in his needy state. Thus the Creator God is invisible, but the needy God is visible. But the needy God becomes visible only when needy people are looked at not through one's external physical eye with but through one's inner spiritual eye.

The lesson of the story is clear. The most notable characteristic of those who are truly noble is their ability to read the anxiety that is in the heart of another and be selflessly a source of relief to that person. Concern for others is such a difficult quality to achieve, that those who have it can be said to be in possession of all other qualities that true religiousness stands for.

This becomes evident to one who can read between the lines of Jesus' story. The supreme judge is not shown here inquiring whether a person is baptized or not. He does not seem to care whether the person to be admitted to the Kingdom is Hindu, Buddhist, Muslim or agnostic. The quality he focuses attention on is that of caring for the needy.

The story is no doubt disturbing for those who uphold that there is no salvation outside the Church. But probably there is no other parable that could indicate with as much clarity what, in Jesus' view true religion and true Christianity will have to be.

The three teachings of Jesus outlined above, show clearly the nature of the mental liberation and the spiritual nobility he wanted to impart to his Jewish listeners. He wanted to enlighten their minds so that they could live their lives at a supra-terrestrial divine level.

---

[14] Mt 25:31-40

Chapter 5
Paul, The Formulator of Multi-Racial Christianity

To understand Christianity and its origins, comprehensively, knowing what Jesus said and did in his lifetime is not enough. This is because during his short 3-4 years of ministry, Jesus had no other aim in view than to bring about a spiritual revival in the Jewish community. If he selected a group of Apostles it was only to help him in that particular task. That is why he ordered them clearly not to go outside the Jewish community or to preach to outsiders whom the Jews called "gentiles".

Do not take the road to gentile lands and do not enter any Samaritan town, but rather go to the lost sheep of the house of Israel.[1]

In the same way as he did, he wanted his apostles too to be throughout their life missionaries exclusively to the Jewish people. But somebody could intervene here, and object to that statement saying that, according to the Gospels, Jesus also told:

Go forth therefore and make all nations my disciples.... and teach them to observe all that I have commanded you.[2]

There is not the least doubt that those words are in the Gospels. But that command is not one he is said to have given during his lifetime but after his resurrection from the dead. Though set in a supra-earthly and fairy-tale type of setting we cannot deny that this assertion was meant to fulfill a much needed purpose. In a way that may astound anybody, not long after the death of Jesus there was a multi-racial group of people who professed that they were believers in the teachings of Jesus. This is what eventually turned out to be the "Christian Church".

But in the Jewish context notably intolerant of other races the chances of getting such an organization accepted was minimal. So there was a need to show everybody that this multi-racial Christian organization did not go against the intention of Jesus and that in fact it was something done in fulfillment of an express order from him. To show this idea convincingly to simple folk there was no better way than to show these words as coming out of the mouth of Jesus himself.

---

[1] Mt. 10 5-6
[2] Mt. 28: 19-20

He had only one simple message for both the Jews and the non-Jews. In simple words, it is this: Salvation or humanness of the noblest form is achieved not by belonging to one or another race, but by the life-long effort to fulfill the will of God, or more tangibly, the dictates of one's conscience.

But the origin of Christianity as a multi-racial religion cannot be understood if we do not take into consideration the life and activities of a rather strange individual called Paul. To give an idea of who he is we give below two key aspects of his life and mission. They are first the gruesome struggle he had to wage to make Christianity a multi-racial religion, and second the elements of the inner character that he wanted a genuine Christian to be adorned with.

68. Paul's Struggle with Christianity

It could surprise anybody to hear that after Jesus, the person most spoken of in the New Testament is Paul. The larger part of the New Testament is not just of him but also by him. There is in it even an entire book on him called the "Acts of the Apostles". Going by the title, the book should be a record of the activities of, if not all the apostles, at least of most of them. But the "apostle" it talks of almost exclusively is not one of the twelve, but Paul, a convert to Christianity after the death of Jesus. Of the 28 chapters in it, 23 are dedicated to his life and activities. The 13 letters written by him included in the New Testament are further proof of the struggle he waged in the establishment of the early Church.

According to "Acts"[3], at its most initial level, the Christian Church was inaugurated during the Jewish festival of Pentecost, a harvest festival of thanksgiving held exactly fifty days after the Pasch. It was at the preceding Pasch that the Jewish priestly authorities had got Jesus condemned to death. On that Pentecostal day when the apostles were assembled together in one room, the Spirit of God descended upon them like "tongues of fire that dispersed among them and rested on each one". Strengthened by the experience, Peter, along with the other disciples, came out to preach to the people about Jesus. Those who listened to them and accepted the message "were baptized and some three thousand were added to their number that day."

---

[3] Acts 2: 1-41

The lesson of the story, though composed in a legendary style is clear. The Church is the work of the Spirit, the Life-power of God. When Jesus, after baptism by John, stepped out of the water to inaugurate his preaching ministry, the Spirit came down on him too. But that was in the form of a dove.

The story also throws light on the type of individuals who formed the early Christian community. The first three thousand were from those who had come to participate in the Jewish Festival of Pentecost, all devotees of the Jewish faith. Some of them were converts to Judaism who were called "proselytes" (literally "alien residents") or just "God-fearers". This is because the Jews granted a subsidiary type of membership to the "gentiles" who accepted to lay aside their cultural traditions and adhere to Jewish customs beginning with circumcision. It was among such people, namely Jews and proselytes that Christianity first originated.

Christianity started as a branch or sect of Judaism. Christians remained adherents of Judaism in all aspects except in the devotion to their teacher, Jesus whom they regarded as the "Christ", the long awaited liberator of the Jews. They went for worship in the temple. As Acts says, "with one mind they kept up their attendance at the temple"[4]. But that situation couldn't last long. The Jewish leaders who had got Jesus condemned to death, wouldn't treat his followers differently. So there was nothing abnormal in their insisting that the doors of the temple be closed to the new sect and that, if possible, the sect be exterminated.

The Christian community had to face up to the situation and start re-organizing itself. It had first of all to select the right shape that the Church as an independent organization should take. Two viewpoints came to the forefront. The larger number felt that after becoming an independent organization, they should keep up the ancestral Jewish traditions. Non-Jewish converts should be made to undergo circumcision. Since Jews were God's chosen people and salvation had to come only through affiliation with them, it had to be so. The proponents of that view were called the "Judaizers".

The other group, more far-seeing but certainly less numerous realized that this procedure, while being an obstacle to the expansion of Christianity, would – and this was what was primary – not be in keeping with the version of religion that Jesus upheld. According to

---

[4] Acts 2: 46

him, salvation could be achieved by anybody who adhered to right life-values, irrespective of race or culture. Therefore they were strongly of the opinion that no Jewish cultural practices should be imposed on converts. Newcomers should be free to retain their cultural traditions. They must only follow the life of the Spirit. Those who upheld that view were called "anti-Judaizers".

According to the picture of the early Church given by the New Testament, there is not the least doubt that the battle between Judaizers and anti-Judaizers was a major issue in it. That was the state in which Christianity was when Paul joined it.

Before starting to examine how Paul joined Christianity and what he did to reshape it, we need to get some idea of his earlier life. Some facts of his life are bound to shock any new student of Christianity. Paul is today called an "apostle" and is ranked as the apostle next to Peter the chief of the apostolic team trained by Jesus. But Paul had no personal contact with Jesus whatsoever. He had never seen him nor heard him. This is because his residence was not in Judea but in Tarsus, a port city of Turkey.

Before he entered Christianity he had been an ardent Jew. For him Judaism was the only true religion, and the Jewish people the only race chosen by Almighty God to be members of his Kingdom. There was no salvation to anybody who was not a member of the Jewish race.

From the moment he heard of the Jewish sect called "Christian" which admitted into it individuals from other races, he began to burn with anger and was determined to exterminate the sect. Equipped with permits from Jewish leaders he began going in search of them and killing them.

But somehow or other all of a sudden, and in a way difficult to explain, his vision changed. According to Acts, the change took place after a vision that Paul (earlier called Saul) had of Jesus when, equipped with letters of authorization from the Jewish priests, he was going to Damascus to destroy the Christians.

While he was still on the road and nearing Damascus, suddenly a light flashed from the sky all around him. He fell to the ground and heard a voice saying, "Saul, Saul, why do you persecute me? "Tell me Lord" he said, "Who are you?" The voice answered, "I am Jesus whom you are persecuting".[5]

---

[5] Acts 9: 1-5

Whatever the reality behind this vision be, there is not the least doubt that at some moment connected with his campaign against Christians he underwent an unbelievable change of heart. It is however not impossible that the question of Jesus "Why do you persecute me?" could have been aroused in his mind by the last words of Christians whom he was putting to death. Acts narrates an incident where he is seen directing the stoning to death of a Christian named Stephen.

The witnesses laid their coats at the feet of a young man named Saul. So they stoned Stephen, and as they did so he called out "Lord Jesus, receive my spirit". Then he fell on his knees and cried aloud "Lord, do not hold this sin against them" and with that he died. And Saul was among them who approved of his murder.[6]

Paul got Stephen killed because he had spoken derogatorily of Judaism. He had said that people did not need the Jewish temple to reach God for, according to the Bible itself, God could be met anywhere under the heavens or on the earth. Judging from his sermon, it seems likely that Stephen was a Christian who belonged to the anti-Judaizer few. It is not impossible that his sermon would have gone a long way to enlighten Paul.

Paul is believed to have been born about 10 AD. If his conversion took place as generally assumed about 36 AD, (that is about 6 years after the death of Jesus) he was about 26 at the time he came to a right vision of religion.

In the first 26 years of his life, he had practiced his religion in the same fanatical manner in which believers of any religion practice the religion they are born in. For them, their religion was the only true religion, and all other religions were false; and so if possible they had to be done away with.

According to Acts, Paul understood the right form of religion only after he pondered over Jesus" question "Saul, Saul, why do you persecute me?" What the question implied was something like this: You persecute me thinking that I am against Judaism. I am not against Judaism. I am against only the clan- protecting form of Judaism but not its personality-building form. Isn't that the Judaism of the deeper form, the Judaism that is of value to the whole of humanity?

That question contained all the religious instruction he needed. In understanding what Judaism is in its universally adaptable

---

[6] Acts 7: 58-8:17

dimension, he had met Jesus face to face. Paul did not want to know anything more about Jesus. As he says in his Epistle to the Ephesians:

It was by a revelation that his secret was made known to me. I have already written a brief account of this, and by reading it you may perceive that I understood the secret of Christ. In former generations this was not disclosed to the human race; but now it has been revealed by inspiration to his dedicated apostles and prophets that through the Gospel, the Gentiles are joint heirs with the Jews, part of the same body, sharers together in the promise made in Christ Jesus. Such is the Gospel of which I was made a minister by God's gift bestowed unmerited on me.[7]

The new truth that he discovered and which he called the "secret of Christ" is that "the Gentiles are joint heirs with the Jews, part of the same body". Many of us today find it difficult to understand what the "secret of Christ" implies because the word "gentiles" does not strike us with the same force it did Paul. For him "gentiles" (as also its equivalent "uncircumcised") referred to all in the world who are not racially Jews. "Gentiles" would thus today include the Chinese and the Africans, the Hindus and the Buddhists.

This conviction of Paul that salvation or humanness of the highest stature is achievable by people of all regions and religions, – a conviction that Christian Theology of today, being institution-protective will find difficult to concede to – is what compelled Paul to join the anti-Judaizer group when he entered the Church. When Paul entered the Church, a number of non-Jews had been admitted into it on the condition that they adhere to the cultural traditions proper to the Jewish people.

Paul knew of this method of admission and the support it received from the Church leaders. That is why he decided to launch out his own campaign of conversion and create anew a genuinely multi-racial version of Christianity without even consulting the Church leaders.

Without Circumcision

Of the Jewish customs imposed on the converts, the one that was considered the most compulsory, and for the converts the most cumbersome was circumcision. It involved surgery on the sex organ of the male. Paul started admitting non-Jews to Christianity without

---

[7] Ephes. 3: 3-7

circumcision. With such uncircumcised Christians, he built up many communities.

His reason for going against the accepted custom is simple. If non-Jewish converts to Christianity had to subscribe to Jewish cultural traditions simply because Christianity originated in a Jewish culture, there was something wrong somewhere. Paul saw where the mistake was. People unduly linked religion with culture and made religion subservient to it. So, according to him, if Christianity as a vision of life was to be adopted by people of all clans and cultures, it had to be above culture or supra-cultural.

But with regard to this approach to the diffusion of Christianity, Paul–and this is what many Christian devotees could find disturbing– had trouble with the Church leaders most of whom were still the apostles. What could seem worse, he had difficulties even with Peter the chief of the apostles, the one considered the head of the Church. Peter, the first pope according to Christians of the Catholic tradition, though a little impulsive at times, was a genuinely gracious man and an un-ostentatious leader. But, like for most human beings, it was not easy for him to change the ideas he had been brought up in. He had been taught from childhood that only his race was pure and so he, as a member of that race, could not share a meal with those who were uncircumcised.

In the case of Peter, something happened which was meant to open his eyes. He was given a vision, a somewhat strange one, to discover the truth.[8] He was presented with a vessel that contained all kinds of animals some of whom according to Jewish criteria were pure and others impure. Peter was asked to use all of them for his food. Peter refused to make use of those considered impure. A voice from heaven was then heard by him: "It is not for you to call impure what God considers pure". Peter understood the message. The distinction between pure and impure whether in animals or human beings is a man-made distinction. Peter saw that Chinese, Africans, Indians do not need Jewish circumcision to become clean.

After the vision, Peter, whose family name was "Cephas", was convinced of the truth. But conviction can't change long-standing habits at once. And so, even after the vision, though through no other fault of his than timidity, there was an instance where he couldn't take the right stand. Paul confronted Peter in public when he saw that.

---

[8] Acts 10: 9-16

But when Cephas came to Antioch, I opposed him to his face because clearly he was in the wrong. For until certain persons came from James he was taking his meals with gentile Christians; but when they came he drew back and began to hold aloof, because he was afraid of the advocates of circumcision. The other Jewish Christians showed the same lack of principle;

But when I saw that their conduct did not square with the truth, I said to Cephas before the whole congregation: "If you a Jew, born and bred, live like a gentile and not like a Jew, how can you insist that gentiles must live like Jews?"[9]

In many places the people whom he had admitted to Christianity without circumcision were forced by other Church leaders to undergo circumcision. He warned his converts against getting misled by such preachers. And he did not hesitate to talk out his mind against such misguided preachers who wanted to diffuse their culture under cover of diffusing religion. One of the crudest attacks of Paul on the imposers of circumcision may well be the following contained in the letter he sent to the Philippians. There he calls those who impose circumcision on converts as "dogs".

To repeat what I have written to you before is no trouble to me and it is a safeguard to you. Beware of those dogs and their malpractices. Beware of those who insist on mutilation, – "circumcision" I will not call it. We are the circumcised, we whose worship is spiritual, whose pride is in Christ Jesus, and who put no confidence in anything external.[10]

This statement is sufficient proof that the battle Paul had had to wage is not an easy one. In any case, there is not the least doubt that, if not for Paul, all Christians of today would belong to the category of the circumcised.

Council of Jerusalem

We may say that Paul succeeded to a large extent in getting his idea accepted by the Church authorities. When his endeavors met with serious opposition and led to major controversies in both Jerusalem and Antioch, Paul appealed to the Church leaders, mainly Peter, the chief of the apostles and James the Bishop of Jerusalem to take a stand. The decision taken at the council [11] convened for the purpose in

---

[9] Gal. 2: 11-14
[10] Phil. 3: 1-3

Jerusalem – the first of the numerous ecumenical councils in Christianity's history – shows that not only Peter but even James who had originally been doubtful about the rectitude of Paul's approach, had come to accept that his vision was in keeping with the idea of Jesus.

The fact that Paul fought against the imposition of circumcision on converts to Christianity should not, of course, make one think that this was all he was concerned about. His real fight was for the right pattern that missionaries should follow when diffusing Christianity. A religion has to be diffused for the vision of life and right living it upholds. A vision loses its spirit as also the power to transform people internally when controlled by a culture. Further people of any clan or culture should be in a position to enhance the vision provided by a religion without having to give up their culture. Therefore what missionaries should diffuse, according to him, are values and not the culture of any one particular community.

For a fuller understanding of the missionary principle that Paul defended, we must look at the Christian values he wanted the converts to adhere to. That should be the most important part in any study of Paul. But before we go to that, we feel a word of caution would be in place to prospective readers of Paul's writings as to how these should be understood. This is because there seem to be many today who have difficulties in getting a realistic view of Paul's concept of Christianity.

Pauline Language

Paul's writings have certainly a complex side to them. Complexities are unavoidable in literature coming down from ancient times. This is particularly applicable to religious literature. Since religions deal with spiritual matters such as life-values and matters dealing with personality-transformation which are beyond the grasp of the physical senses, religions have no alternative but to use symbolic language. They cannot use the language of news-papers, novels and school text-books.

They have to make use of symbols of supra-terrestrial images to make the realities they describe easy enough for ordinary folk and especially the illiterate to understand. But the thoughtful believer should know how to subscribe to the deep spiritual lesson leaving out

---

[11] Acts 15:3-35

the legend that envelops it. He should also not fail to keep an eye on the goal that the religious writer is trying to achieve by what he says.

Of the numerous issues of that type in the writings and teachings of Paul, we can take just one for examination, namely, what he says about Jesus. Though he had never met Jesus personally, he was astounded by the extra-ordinary lesson Jesus had taught about the universality of salvation. That teaching of Jesus was so powerful that it changed Paul's entire attitude to life and religion.

We should of course not make the mistake of thinking that the principle of universal salvation was an idea initiated by Jesus. It was a principle ingrained in the plan of God from eternity. God wanted all human beings without exception to achieve humanness of the noblest form. But Jesus is the one who vividly reminded the Jewish people of that divine plan. It was to express impressively the value of what Jesus did, that Paul exalted the individuality of Jesus, to the stature of a super-human divine being. That is how he referred to Jesus as "Son of God".

Nobody can question Paul's statement that Jesus is the "Son of God". But that statement should be correctly understood. His divinity is not something inherited, in which case Jesus should have existed with God eternally even before the creation of the world. Such an assumption would go against the monotheism of the Judeo-Christian Bible. The divinity of Jesus is what he acquired on earth after his birth from Mary and Joseph by living a life in accordance with the Spirit of God.

There is a great likelihood that later Christians have not been able to decipher correctly what Paul said of Jesus. It is not impossible that it is a misunderstanding of Pauline language that has compelled institutionalized Christian Churches of a later era to include into their creeds the idea that Jesus is one of the members of the "Three-person God" or the "Trinity". Such an interpretation would go against the intention of Jesus to make all human beings sons and daughters or children of God.

But Paul's reference to Jesus as "Son of God" should not make us conclude that Paul ignored at any moment that Jesus was fully a human being as any of us. We can cite one brief text in which in one line he refers to Jesus as "Son of God" and in another as the brother of James, the Christian bishop of Jerusalem at that time. If Jesus was the brother of James, he was as human as James. The text is one in which he explains why after entering Christianity and starting his own group of Christians, he avoided going to see the apostles for as long a time as three years.

You have heard what my manner of life was when I was still a practicing Jew: how savagely I persecuted the Church of God and tried to destroy it.... But in his good pleasure God, who had set me apart from birth and called me through his grace, chose to reveal his Son to me and through me, in order that I may proclaim him among the gentiles.....

Three years later, I did go to Jerusalem to get to know Cephas (i.e. Peter). I stayed with him for a fortnight without seeing any other of the apostles except James the Lord's brother. What I write is plain truth; before God, I am not lying.[12]

If Paul spoke of Jesus as the "Son of God" we must not forget that this was because, in the dreadful war he waged almost single-handed with the powerful "Judaizer" group he had a need for doing so. They wanted to thwart his enterprise of admitting non-Jews without circumcision. For them circumcision was indispensable for salvation because it is given in the Law which God gave to the Jewish people. To them his reply was that such a claim was absurd because salvation was not through the Law (the Jewish Bible) but through Jesus. When saying so he took "Jesus the Son of God" as a symbol of the "the eternal principle of God, regarding the universality of salvation". In the way Paul understood Jesus, salvation was available not just to members of the Jewish race, but to all human beings of whatever caste or creed.

69. What it is to be Christian According to Paul

To understand more positively what really Paul taught and fought for, we have to go to the vision he had of Christianity. From his numerous epistles there is one that he has dedicated very specially to teach what the character of a true Christian should be. It is his Epistle to the Romans written around 56-58 AD to a community of Christians in Rome composed of both Jews and non-Jews. It is the teaching of that Epistle that we want to examine here to find out what Paul required of a true Christian. We have however, to restrict ourselves to just a few aspects of Christian spirituality given in it.

---

[12] Gal. 1:13-20

Two Levels of Life

Basic to Paul's thought in this matter is the distinction he makes about the two levels at which an individual can lead his or her life. He calls one the level "of lower nature" and the other the "level of the spirit".

Those who live on the level of our lower nature have their outlook formed by it, and that spells death; but those who live on the level of the spirit have the spiritual outlook, and that is life and peace.

For the outlook of the lower nature is enmity with God; it is not subject to the law of God; indeed it cannot be; those who live on such a level cannot possibly please God. But that is not how you live. You are on the spiritual level if only God's Spirit dwells within you.[13]

According to the Bible, The Spirit of God was the life-power or the breath of Almighty God. Since Almighty God was pictured as an unfathomable and humanly inaccessible being, living far away in the heavens (to some extent, like "Brahman" in Hinduism) the Jews introduced the concept of the Spirit of God (like "Atman" in Hinduism) to use when talking of divine activities related to the physical world.

For Paul, the Divine Spirit was what animated, or became the soul of human beings to make them give up their life of low desires and make them live at a divine level of life. Taken in that background, for Paul, the shortest definition of a Christian would be "a person animated by the Spirit of God".

Divine Sonship of Human Beings

According to Paul, the aim of Christianity is to make human beings children of God. "Children" are different from slaves and servants even if they live in the same house. The latter do what they are told out of fear. But children do things spontaneously. They know that they are cared for, wanted and loved. Truly holy people live their lives in a natural spontaneous way. Internally they are happy and in peace.

For all who are moved by the Spirit of God are sons of God. The spirit you have received is not a spirit of slavery leading you back into a life of fear, but a Spirit that makes us sons, enabling us to cry "Abba, father"! In that cry the Spirit of God joins with our spirit in

---

[13] Rom 8:5-9

testifying that we are God's children; and if children then heirs. We are God's heirs and Christ's fellow heirs, if we share his sufferings now in order to share his splendor hereafter"[14]

When talking of spirituality, or the pattern of living, which we call "Christian-ness", what matters for Paul is the Spirit. Just as Jesus was the Son of God because God's spirit was in him, all human beings of whatever clan and culture will be children of God if the Spirit of God is in them.

Right Attitude of Mind

For Paul, Christian-ness is not in the performance of rites but in right living. Worship and sacrifice have to be lived. Religion is an attitude of mind. Paul's simple advice is "Let your minds be re-made".

Therefore my brothers, I implore you by God's mercy to offer your very selves to him: a living sacrifice, dedicated and fit for his acceptance, the worship offered by mind and heart. Adapt yourself no longer to the pattern of this present world but let your minds be remade and your whole nature thus transformed. Then you will be able to discern the will of God and know what is good, acceptable and perfect.[15]

Paul may not be the only person to see the essence of religion as "remaking the mind", For the Buddha too the heart of religion was "reorienting the disoriented mind".

Sense of Responsibility

According to Paul, to be Christian is also to understand one's role in society and execute that role with a sense of responsibility. The profession carried out or the position held is not of much consequence. What is important is that it be fulfilled correctly with a sense of humility and responsibility. For Paul religion is not primarily in asceticism and monasticism but in executing secular duties in a spirit of enlightened dedication.

The gifts we possess differ as they are allotted to us by God's grace, and must be exercised accordingly: the gift of inspired utterance, for example in proportion to a man's faith; or the gift of

---

[14] Rom 8:14-17
[15] Rom 12:1-2

administration, in administration. A teacher should employ his gift in teaching, and one who has the gift of stirring speech should use it to stir his hearers. If you give to charity, give with all your heart. If you are a leader, exert yourself to lead; if you are helping others in distress, do it cheerfully.[16]

Political Duties

Human beings live in a political society. Society needs a governing authority. Citizens of a nation have the obligation to fulfill their duties by the nation with due submission to the governing authority. Correct fulfillment of political duties is a Christian responsibility.

There is no authority but by act of God, and the existing authorities are instituted by him......That is why you are obliged to submit. It is an obligation imposed not merely by fear of retribution, but by conscience. That is also why you pay taxes. The authorities are in God's service and to these duties they devote their energies.[17]

When Paul wrote this letter, Christianity was still a forbidden religion. Being a Christian was a criminal offense for which execution was the penalty. As a matter of fact Paul ended his life as a martyr four or five years later around 62 AD during the reign of Emperor Nero. For Paul to have reminded Christians to fulfill their obligations to their countries even under persecution shows the importance he attached to civic obligations.

Respect for Other Cultures

When Paul wrote his letter to the Romans, controversies had cropped up in the Roman community that could have created irreparable splits in it. One was the question of vegetarianism and non-vegetarianism in food habits. Jews ate meat. But there were converts from other nationalities and religions who practiced abstinence from meat. Then there was also the difference of the weekly rest-day. The Jews celebrated the Saturday, the Sabbath. Converts from other religions didn't care for the Saturday.

The stand Paul takes here is decisive. His solution is the right selection of priorities. In primary matters all must conform. In matters

---

[16] Rom 12:6-8
[17] Rom 13: 1-6

of secondary importance differences should be permitted and the very differences should be made use of for deepening love and respect for each other.

If a man is weak in faith, you must accept him without attempting to settle doubtful points. For instance one man may have faith enough to eat all kinds of food, while a weaker man eats only vegetables....

Again this man regards one day more highly than another, while another man regards all days alike....

Let us therefore cease judging one another, but rather make this simple judgment: that no stumbling block be placed in a brother's way...for the kingdom of God is not eating and drinking, but justice, peace and joy inspired by the Holy Spirit.

Let us then pursue the things that make for peace and build up the common life.[18]

Love Above All

The points mentioned above should give some idea of what Paul understood by Christianity. For him, Christianity stood for Christian character. To conclude our analysis of Paul's insights into Christian character there is no better text in the Epistle to the Romans that we could choose than the following which points to the place that charity should have in the life of a Christian – charity even for persecutors.

Call down blessings on your persecutors, – blessings not curses. With the joyful be joyful and mourn with the mourners. Care as much about each other as about yourselves. Do not be haughty, but go with humble folk. Do not keep thinking how wise you are.

Never pay back evil for evil. Let your aims be such as all men count honorable. If possible, so far as it lies with you, live at peace with all men. My dear friends, do not seek revenge, but leave a place for divine retribution; for there is a text which reads "Justice is mine, says the Lord, I will repay".

He who loves his neighbor has satisfied every claim of the law. For the commandments, "Thou shall not commit adultery, thou shall not kill, thou shall not steal, thou shall not covet" and any other commandment there may be, are all summed up in the one rule, "Love your neighbor as yourself. "Love cannot wrong a neighbor. Therefore the whole law is summed up in love.[19]

---

[18] Rom 14: 1 19

With those insights of Paul into Christian spirituality, we come to the end of this section dedicated to the analysis of Christianity along with Judaism. In this section we have kept to the essence of original Christianity and its link with Judaism as given in the sacred scriptures. That Biblical aspect of Christianity is what a new student, whether Christian or non-Christian, has obligatorily to be acquainted with.

---

[19] Rom 12: 14-21; 13: 8-10

World Religions
Part Four
Islam

Chapter 1
Muhammad, the Founder of Islam

Islam is one of the major religions of the modern world. With nearly 1150 million followers, its membership today is approximately one sixth of the world's population.

The founder of Islam is Muhammad (or Mohammed). He is said to have been born in 570 AD. If so, his appearance in the world would be approximately six centuries after Jesus, the founder of Christianity, just as that of Gautama, the founder of Buddhism was six centuries before Jesus.

70. The Term "Islam"

"Islam", the Arabic term Muhammad used to designate his religion means "submission" or "surrender to the will of God". As explained earlier, the term "God" or "Almighty God" used by Muhammad is the term that Moses of Judaism and Jesus of Christianity too adopted to depict the mysterious divine power that governs all living and non-living entities in the universe and even elsewhere. If all teachers of monotheistic religions have presented God, in the picture of a living person, it is because they would not have seen any other way to make that un-describable divine power imaginable and at least to some extent understandable to ordinary human beings.

If that picture can be considered justifiable, and even indispensable then the term "Islam" meaning "submission to the will of God" is a very apt pointer to the spiritual essence of the religion that Muhammad founded. If translated into secular terminology "submission to the will of God" could be close in meaning to "a life committed to right life-values".

71. Early Life

Muslim devotees address Muhammad through the term "prophet", a term used in Judaism too, or through the Arabic word "Nabi" which means "a Messenger of God" or "one who speaks in the name of God".

Muhammad was by race and nationality Arab. He was born in Mecca a hot dry valley between hills in the middle west of Arabia nearly 110 kilometers from the red sea. Mecca was a well known city on the route in which big caravans travelled from Yemen to Syria. It was also the city in which the Kaaba shrine and the Zamzam well were situated. In Arabic "Kaaba" means a cube or a block of six almost equal square sides.

In one wall of the Kaaba shrine was fixed a big black stone widely believed to be a meteorite fallen from the sky. People coming from all parts of Arabia to worship it, had made Mecca a centre of pilgrimage from very ancient times.

According to one legend connected with Muhammad's birth, an angel had announced to his mother that she was going to be the prophet's mother. According to another, a blood stained sin-clot was removed from his body when he was a child.

Muhammad's father and mother bore the names of Abdulla and Amina. His father died before he was born. Mother died when he was just six years. After his mother's death he was looked after by his grandfather. He too died after two years. It is not impossible that what made him contemplate about life and its purpose would have been such unfortunate experiences in his early life. After his grandfather's death, he came under the protection of his uncle, Abu Talib.

In early life, like all other people of Arabia Muhammad too associated the Kaaba. But the type of worship conducted there, did not appeal to him. He resented the polytheistic trends of the rituals performed there.

Since the main source of livelihood in Mecca was trade, Muhammad too engaged in trade activities. From his childhood, with his uncle, he joined caravans that carried goods for trade. It is said that at the age of twelve he joined his uncle leading a caravan to Syria situated to the north of Mecca.

72. Marriage to Kadija

At the age of 25 he acquired a job under a rich lady called Kadija. She owned a number of caravans. With those caravans he often went to the main cities of Syria. To get an idea of the wider world, those trips were of immense help to him. He got a chance thereby to converse with people with diverse ideas. He met people who followed religions like Christianity, Judaism and Zoroastrianism. He was much impressed by the monotheistic ideas held by them.

According to a widely accepted early tradition, he had built up a close friendship with a Christian hermit.

Kadija was older to Mohammed by a number of years. But he got attracted to her and eventually married her. He got seven children from her. While he was married to her, he did not keep any other wife.

73. Life of Meditation

As the husband of Kadija he did not have to labor for a living. He had as a result much free time to reflect restfully on what he had seen and heard. Since he had a natural inclination for meditation he often went into a cave situated in Mecca itself to reflect in solitude on matters pertaining to life and living.

Why do Arab people worship images made of clay, stone and wood? Why don't they like Jews and Christians worship one, universal, almighty being that cannot be rendered in pictures and images? There is no doubt that, questions such as these would have formed the main subject of his meditations.

Once when he was engaged in meditation in the cave an angel is said to have accosted him and spoken to him of a holy book enshrined in heaven from time immemorial. After that the angel had recited some extracts from it and requested Muhammad to repeat them aloud after him. Though Muhammad had not learned to read and write, he could say correctly what he was asked to say.

The fact that Muhammad could not read and write does not mean that he was an uneducated man. In Arabia of that early era, the ability to read and write was not very common. In jobs related to trade for example, literacy was not considered an obligatory requirement. Further, literacy was necessary for knowledge in physical sciences. But Muhammad was not in the realm of science, but of religion. What is required for religion is insight or inspiration. Insight is gained through meditation. In his meditations, inspiration came to him through what are referred to as angelic apparitions.

After receiving a number of such angelic apparitions, he became convinced that he was entrusted with the task of teaching the people around him of the supreme almighty God and liberating them from their polytheistic beliefs in gods and goddesses. He felt that he was called to become the Prophet of "Allah". "Allah" is the common Arabic term for "Almighty God".

But at the beginning he kept silent about the apparitions and the enlightenment he got through them about the manner in which his prophetic task had to be executed. He divulged them only to a small number of close acquaintances. His wife Kadija believed in his apparitions. A faithful assistant of his called Zaid, a cousin brother called Ali, and a respected individual named Abu Bakr also believed in him. They became also his first followers. Ali and Abu Bakr became governors of Islam after Muhammad.

74. Conflicts at Start of Mission

Muhammad was determined to engage in the mission of introducing to the people of Arabia the idea of one supreme God. To execute that task Kadija gave him all the help and encouragement. It was then that Muhammad started preaching the religion of Islam to the Arab people.

He first went to the residents of Mecca and asked them to submit to the will of Allah. A few listened to him and accepted his teachings. But the majority was reluctant to give up their polytheistic traditions they were, for ages, used to. They resented his preaching campaign and started to persecute his followers. Because of that, a number of his followers fled across the red sea to Ethiopia inhabited by a large number of Christians.

At that time it came to light that some Meccans were plotting to kill him. Muhammad felt that the time had come for him to get out of Mecca. In 622 he left his place of birth and fled to Medina a city situated 320 kilometers to the north of Mecca. Medina (earlier called Yathrib) is the name that the city got after his arrival there. It means "the city of the Prophet". The flight of Muhammad is called "Hijra" (literally "migration"). The year in which the "Hijra" took place is considered the first year of the Muslim calendar. All the years after that are numbered with the addition of the two letters "AH", the initials from the Latin term "Anno Hijra".

There were numerous Jewish groups in Medina. Since like them he too advocated monotheism, and because he had a great regard for the Jewish Bible and the Jewish prophets, he expected that they would offer their cooperation to him. But what happened was the opposite. The Jews did not tolerate him. He got an inkling that they were even plotting to kill him. Because of that he drove some of the Jews out of Medina and even killed some of them.

It was then that he came to the conclusion that a holy war, called in Arabic "Jihad", should be waged to establish his religion in his land. On one occasion when his followers were short of food he attacked a caravan coming from Mecca carrying foodstuff. When the leaders of Mecca got news of the attack they dispatched an army of 900 men to Medina. Muhammad with just 300 men defeated them. Thereafter a bigger army was sent to Medina. They inflicted heavy damage to Muhammad's party but still they could not snatch the city from Muhammad's control. Muhammad was a person highly talented in matters of warfare.

From then onwards he began to gain victory step by step. As soon as he had established his battling power, he sent an army to Mecca. In 630 without any opposition Mecca surrendered to his army. When the city became calm, he went to Mecca and began cleansing it. He destroyed all the polytheistic idols that were in the Kaaba shrine. It is said that he abstained from destroying an image of Jesus and of mother Mary. He then invited all the inhabitants of the city to the Kaaba for the worship of the one and only almighty God who cannot be rendered in images. He told them to give up idolatry and be just and honest and not to take revenge from enemies. After thus establishing his control over Mecca he went back to his home in Medina.

From then onwards the Kaaba temple encasing the black stone became the main place of worship of the Muslims. Until that time it had been the custom of Muslims to turn to Jerusalem, the sacred city of the Jews when performing acts of worship. After the conquest of Mecca they started the new custom of turning to Mecca when saying prayers. Today Muslims of any part of the world turn to Mecca when they pray.

75. Respect for Other Religions

Muhammad always respected the religious traditions of the Jews as also of the Christians. He also spoke of Jesus with deep respect. He is said to have listened with deep reverence and enthusiasm to two individuals from Abyssinia when they read aloud the Bible and the Gospels.

In the same way as the Jews and the Christians, he accepted Abraham as the father of monotheism. He claimed that his main task was to conserve till the end of time the monotheism started ages ago by Abraham. He always looked at himself as a prophet walking in the steps of Moses who taught the divine law to the Jews and of Jesus who taught the Gospel (Good News) to the Christians. What he considered his main task was introducing the monotheism of the Jews and the Christians to his people who were Arab.

Prophet Muhammad had nine wives. Polygamy was not a practice uncommon to Arab people or even the Jews. The great Jewish king David too is said to have had many wives. Muhammad had a great desire to have a son. But he was unfortunate not to have a member of his progeny to take over the reins of Islam after him. After fleeing to Medina, Muhammad lived only for ten years. He ended his life in 630 AD due to an intestinal ailment. He died at the age of 62 in the house of his most cherished wife Aisha who was also the daughter of Abu Bakr. During his lifetime he was successful in unifying all the tribes of Arabia under the Islamic flag.

After Muhammad, Abu Bakr took over the control of Islam. Muhammad is considered by his followers as the main prophet of God as also his last prophet. They believe that it is his task to take all human beings to the presence of God.

76. Two Questions Posed, First About Monotheism

Before we conclude this chapter, it may not be out of place to pose for reflection two questions commonly raised by students of Islam. The first is about Islam's relationship to other monotheistic religions. The second is about Islam's engagement in warfare. The first question asked is this: If Judaism, Christianity and Islam profess the same form of monotheism, and submit to one and the same God, how is it that they have not been able to join hands together or at least be in close relationship with each other?

The answer to this apparently simple but internally very provocative question lies in the fact that the word "monotheism" as also the word "religion" (which will be explained more in detail in the last section of this book) can be taken in one of two senses, a spiritual sense and an institutional sense.

In the first sense, monotheism is what contributes to an individual's personal spirituality. It induces one to keep united with God in heart, and achieve inner nobility at its highest level. There is not the least doubt that there are many enlightened followers in each of the three religions of Judaism, Christianity and Islam who understand monotheism in that light. They accept truth-loving and so, mentally liberated individuals of all the three communities as their own brothers and sisters and consider them as forming together one spiritual church or one religion of the Spirit.

Taken in the other sense, monotheism is an article of the creed of all the three religions in their institutionalized form. All institutionalized religions are culturally and politically different from one another. Judaism and Islam are clearly so. Christianity too, three centuries after the life of Jesus evolved from a spiritual religion to a politically institutionalized one. In their present culturally and politically diverse form, members of Judaism, Christianity and Islam can in no way get together. They go their own ways in practicing and propagating their institutionalized version of monotheism. More often than not they are in conflict with one another. The answer to that first question is thus clear and short. Monotheism of the spiritual form can unite the three religions. That of the institutionalized form cannot.

77. Second Question: Islam's Religious Warfare

The second question asked about Islam by non-Muslims, and which could sound even more hurtful, is this: Isn't Islam a religion that engages in war and converts nations by conquest? Isn't the commitment to Holy War for the protection and propagation of Islam, and technically called "Jihad", prescribed as an obligation of Muslims?

Nobody who looks at the history of Islam can deny that Islamic states have made invasions and converted countries by conquest. Nevertheless conversion by conquest cannot be taken as an activity exclusive to Islam. Any institutionalized religion that is convinced that it is the only true religion in the world will, if politically powerful, engage in wars to convert so-called "pagan" nations. As a matter of fact, Christianity started converting nations to Christianity by conquest long before Islam.

It is not impossible that Islam got the idea of Holy War from Christianity. There is however a difference between the two. In Christianity holy wars started long after the life of the Founder; in Islam during the life of the Founder himself.

Being a deep visionary, there is no doubt that Muhammad would have always taken "Submission to the will of God" or "Islam" as the path that individuals had to follow to achieve humanness of the fullest and eternally lasting form. But he could also have felt that for individuals to live in submission to God, an Islamic social environment would be helpful. That could be why he decided that, as far as possible entire nations should be compelled to follow an Islamic pattern of regime. Whatever the reason be, among the religions of today, Islam is the religion that has spread out the fastest. The extent of Islam in the modern world is hard to estimate. It stretches from Senegal to Mongolia and from Russia to South Africa.

Chapter 2
Koran (Al-Quran) the Sacred Text of the Muslims

The sacred text of the Muslims is the Koran or in Arabic the "Al-Qur an". The meaning of that word is "what is recited" which is suggestive of the fact that it is composed of texts which were first recited than written down. The Koran contains what was revealed to Muhammad over a period of twenty years by God through the angel "Gibril" (in Christianity "Gabriel"). The text is also supposed to be based on a book enshrined in heaven from time immemorial. The Koran was delivered to Muhammad in the Arabic language.

78. Composition of the Koran

Since Muhammad could not read and write, it is not treated as a book composed by him. Soon after his death, the first "Calif" or the governor of Islam ordered a faithful scribe called Zaid to collect the revelations to Muhammad recorded in scraps of material including bones of camels, and very especially those preserved in the memory of his close followers, and to compose the first version of the Koran. The collection is believed to have been completed around the year 650.

About 20 years after the first edition, Uthman, the third Calif seeing that there were diverse versions of the Koran in circulation, got the same Zaid to prepare anew a final edition to be considered authoritative. He sent copies of the final edition to all the cities and got the variations destroyed. As a result, today there is only one authentic version of the Koran.

The Koran is not a book that is easy for an ordinary person to read at once and understand. The main reason is that it is composed in rhythmic prose and in lines of uneven length. Further it is a book meant to be learnt by heart and chanted uniformly together. Because of the rhythmic tone intrinsic to the wording, the texts in it are not easy to translate.

Another difficulty in reading it comes from the way that the chapters are arranged. After the first chapter, called the "Fatiha" (opening) which contains a prayer for guidance, all the chapters are arranged according to their length. The longer chapters are put at the beginning and the shorter ones at the end. Thus the second chapter consists of 386 verses. Chapter 110 has only 3 lines. In English translations (See: Everyman in Penguin series) this order has been reverted. In them the shorter ones are at the beginning. This makes it easier for an ordinary person to read.

Muslim devotees, – even those whose mother-tongue is not Arabic – learn the Koran only in Arabic. At least the prayers and the short chapters they learn by heart. The Koran is not a very big book. It is not bigger than the New Testament of the Christians. The Buddhist Dhammapada is at least three times the size of the Koran.

There are in all 114 chapters in the Koran. The name for "chapter" in Arabic is "surah". Above some chapters, the title given is "Mecca", and above others, "Medina". The title indicates the place where Muhammad received the revelation. He was in Mecca from 610 AD to 622 and in Medina from 622 to 632. The greater number of the short "surahs" was recited by him at the instigation of the angel when he was in Mecca. Though short, they are very powerful. They speak of the oneness of God and include injunctions to his followers to serve God faithfully and to abandon the worship of false gods. The chapters which belong to the Medina section are long. Most of them deal with the Muslim society system. They contain directions for the solution of problems such as those arising from ownership of property, poverty, employment, politics and war.

Every chapter of the Koran, except one, opens with the words "In the name of the most kind and most compassionate God". In most chapters, God is described as the supreme judge. But everywhere the emphasis is on his love and compassion.

In the translated versions of the Koran, the chapters are numbered as in ordinary books with figures such as 1, 2, 3. But in the Arabic edition, the chapters are named using names such as "Abraham", "Joseph", "Mary", "Cow", "Bee" and "Unity".

Muhammad presented the Koran to his people as a book revealed by God. But he did not hesitate to recognize the sacred books of the Jews and the Christians too as revelations of God. He called the three communities of Jews, Christians and Muslims by the name of "Peoples of the book". He often reminded his followers to respect the sacred books of the Jews and the Christians.

Most revered leaders of the Bible are mentioned in the Koran. Even though with minor variations, what is said of them in the Bible is repeated in the Koran. Adam, Abraham (Ibrahim) Joseph, David, Solomon are presented in the Koran as prophets who conveyed the message of God.

Jesus is very respectfully mentioned over twenty times in the Koran. The story of the birth of Jesus from the Virgin Mary is narrated twice almost in the same words as those given in the Gospel of Luke. The Last Supper of Jesus too is mentioned in it. It rejects however the crucifixion story. This is because Muhammad was of the view that God could not have submitted a saintly person like Jesus to such an abominable death. But he accepted the resurrection of Jesus and his ascension to heaven.

Since the Koran upheld a strict version of monotheism he rejected the Christian belief in the Trinity or the dogma that God consisted of three persons. But the understanding he had of the Trinity is different from the official Christian teaching. He took the Trinity to be composed of Jesus, Mary and Joseph.

Among the non-Muslims, the religion that Muslims consider most akin to them is Christianity. Even though Muhammad excluded monasticism from his religious system he had a great regard for the Christian monks living in the Arabian Desert.

In a number of the short chapters coming at the beginning of the Koran, the judgment of human beings at the end of the world is profusely illustrated. Events like the darkening of the sun and the sky, the resurrection of the dead, the admission of good people to heaven and the expulsion of bad people to hell are shown as events of the final judgment.

Due to special requirements, the Koran permits a Muslim to keep 4 wives. But today most Muslims keep only one wife.

The Koran is Islam's main sacred text. But there is another book that contains Muhammad's teachings and injunctions. It is called the "Hadith", a term meaning "Traditional Beliefs". What is contained in it are not considered divine revelations of God. But since its contents are vital for the solution of the problems that Muslims face in their day to day life, the "Hadith" is considered Islam's second sacred book.

79. Main Beliefs of the Muslims

To get a clearer idea of what the Koran contains, it is useful for us to take a brief glance at the beliefs that it tells the Muslims to obligatorily profess. There are six main beliefs which together are considered the "Foundation of Islam".

In brief they are:

1) There is one divinity controlling the entire universe. He is Allah.
2) There are angels that bring the messages of God from heaven to earth.
3) There are books that contain the messages of God.
4) There are individuals called prophets who are empowered by God to explain the divine messages to human beings.
5) There is at the end of the world a Judgment Day on which all human beings will be rewarded or punished according to what they have done in their lives.
6) Allah controls the entire universe and everything that happens within it.

1. Belief in One God: The heart of the religion of Islam is faith in one God, Allah. God sees everything, hears everything. He is all powerful. He is the supreme authority over the entire universe. He is its creator and protector. There is nobody in heaven or on earth equal to him. Therefore he cannot be rendered in any material images. As the Koran says:

Humans, pray to God who created you and everybody before you. For your residence he created the earth and built the sky over it as a roof. He is the one who, for the purpose of feeding you, sends rain from the bosom of the sky and makes trees bear fruit. Pray to God for your protection. With your knowledge never let a material image be made to represent him (2:21-23).

2. Belief in Angels: According to Muslim understanding, angels are a type of being composed of light. Their leader is called "Gibril". It is he who brought the message of the Koran to Muhammad. There is also an angel expelled from heaven and leads people away from God. He is called "Iblis" or "Shaitan".

3. Sacred Books: Muslims believe that there are four sacred texts that contain messages of the Almighty God. The first is the "Torah" revealed to "Musa" (Moses). That is the initial part of the Jewish-Christian Bible. The second is the Book of Songs "Zabur" revealed to prophet "Davud" (David). It is the Book of Psalms in the

Jewish-Christian Bible. The third is the "Injil" revealed to the prophet "Isa" (Jesus). It is the Gospel of the Christian New Testament.

The last is the main and final revelation, the Koran. The Koran is superior and supersedes all other sacred texts which are not found in their original form any longer. The "Injil" itself went back to heaven with Jesus. Muslims consider the Koran which explains what they have to do from birth till death an astounding divine miracle.

4) Prophets: Muslims believe that there are 124,000 prophets who have fulfilled their task of bringing messages from God to human beings. But only 22 of them are mentioned in the Koran. Of these the ones known to Christians, in their Christian names, are Adam, Noah, Abraham, Moses, David and Jesus. But of all the prophets, Muhammad is the greatest and is also the last prophet. He is described by Muslims as the "Seal of Divine Revelation".

5) Day of Judgment: On a day called the "Day of Final Judgment" God Allah will resurrect the dead from their graves and reward or punish all human beings according to the good or bad they have done in their lifetime. Those who lived with true faith will be admitted to heaven to live joyfully forever. Those who have been unfaithful to their faith will be destined to spend their life painfully in hell.

The ten sins that are considered grave or mortal by Muslims are the following: a) Worship of other gods than Allah, b) Being unfaithful to the fundamental teachings of Islam, c) Falsehood or telling lies d) Sexual misconduct e) Misappropriation of the goods of others, f) Deception and fraud, g) Bearing false witness against the innocent, h) Slander or making false charges, i) Defaming of character, j) Hurting the feelings of others.

6) Divine Control: The last important belief is the one in the power of God to control the world and design everything that happens within it. Nothing happens anywhere without his knowledge. Natural laws regarding breeding and growth of life, changes in seasons and climates are all designed by him. But this divine law does not enslave human beings. It does not imprison the human will. The human will is completely free to choose between right and wrong but, of course, with the responsibility to bear the final consequences for the choice.

What has been said above about the Koran and its teachings should show anybody, particularly a non-Muslim, that as a teacher of religion, Muhammad was a person endowed with an extra-ordinary character. He did not want to hide the fact that in doctrinal matters his Islam depended almost entirely on Judaism and Christianity. He was honest enough to accept that he took most of his religious teachings from those two monotheistic religions. He was also large-hearted and open-minded to show deep respect to those religions and go to the extent of requesting his followers to do the same. If he did not link up with those religions, it is not because of any doctrinal disagreements, but because of institutional requirements.

Muhammad viewed religion as an institution that had a socio-political culture of its own. In his view, Islam as a religion would be better safeguarded if submission to God was supported by submission to political authority. But of course, we must admit that the link between religion and state has both a happy and an unhappy side to it. On the happy side, the link with the state can give the religious community a social and an economic stability. On the unhappy side (as has happened with Christianity) either the religion or the state can split into parts; thereafter each religious sect gets governed by a separate political body.

Chapter 3
Religious Duties of Muslims, the Five Pillars of Islam

There are five duties that any Muslim has obligatorily to fulfill. Since they form the basis of the Muslim institution, they are generally referred to as the "Pillars of Islam". With their Arabic names they are: 1. Profession of Faith (Sahada), 2. Prayer (Salat), 3. Almsgiving (Zakat), 4. Fasting (Sawm), 5. Pilgrimage to Mecca (Hajj). The way they are to be executed is as follows.

80. Profession of Faith (Sahada)

Anybody who wants to become a Muslim must begin by making the Profession of Faith called in Arabic "Sahada". It consists of the words "There is no other God but Allah, and Muhammad is the prophet who proclaims his will to humanity." It serves the same function as the "creed" in all religions but, of all the creeds, it could well be the shortest. Mohammad felt that for people who could not normally read and write a Profession of Faith should be short and intelligible. What the Muslim profession of faith implies is that the believer accepts to do the will of the one and only God in the way the Prophet declared.

81. Daily Worship of God (Salat)

In the way that Muhammad declared was decreed to him by God, a Muslim must worship God five times a day. The times further were unchangeably fixed. They are: a) Dawn (Fajr), b) Midday (Zuhr), c) Afternoon (Asr), d) Sunset (Magrib), and night (Isha). The worship at those fixed times is called "Salat" literally "prayer" and applies particularly to this ritual version of worship.

So as not to leave possibility for the worship to be missed or bypassed, a caller-to-prayer called "Muezzin" was employed to announce whenever the time was right for worship. He made the announcement orally as loudly as possible from a fixed place at the top of a mosque His announcement is called "Azan" and is as follows:

a) "Allahu Akbar". "The only God is Allah". (This is said four times.) (b) "I bear witness that there is no other God but Allah" (said twice). (c) "I bear witness that Muhammad is his Prophet" (twice). (d)

"Come to Prayer" (twice). (e) "Come for protection and security" (twice). (f) "Worship is better than sleep" (said only in the morning). (g) "The only God deserving of worship is Allah" (once).

Preparatory Ablution: As soon as devotees hear this call from the mosque they prepare to pray by performing an ablution for purification. The manner of performing the ablution is outlined in the Koran and consists of six steps. The devotee starts the ablution with the words "in the name of the Almighty and all Compassionate God", and repeats it till the end of the cleaning exercise.

First the hands are washed up to the wrist three times. Second, the devotee must take water into his mouth and wash the mouth. Even a toothbrush could be used for the purpose. Third, he should wash his nostrils three times and also his face three times. Fourth, he should wash his right hand first and then his left hand up to the elbow three times. Fifth, with his wet hands he should brush his head, neck and ears three times. Lastly, he should wash his right leg first and left leg second up to the ankle three times.

Exercise of Worship: The pattern for the performance of the Salat prayer is clearly indicated in the Koran. The exercise at any given time consists of a number of prayer-rounds each called a "Rakah". There are 2 "Rakahs" in the morning, 4 at noon, 4 in the afternoon, 3 at sunset and 4 at night.

Building Bridges

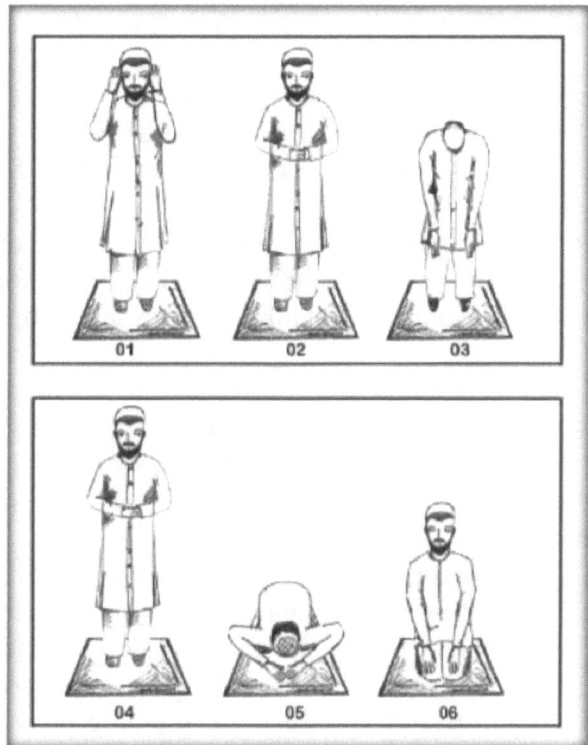

Each "Rakah" or prayer round consists of six distinct gestures. (The six gestures are sketchily portrayed above.) In the first gesture, the devotee lifts the two hands up to the ear keeping the palms facing forward. Holding his hands so, he says "Allahu Akbar" meaning "the only God is Allah".

At the second, he keeps the two hands in front of the stomach and says by heart the first chapter of the Koran called the "Fatiha" of which the words are as follows:

a) In the name of the most kind and most merciful God Allah;
b) In the name of God Allah who protects the entire universe;
c) You who are the master of the last judgment day;
d) We worship you only. We ask assistance only from you.
e) Show us the straight path.
f) Show us the path followed not by those who fight against your will but of those who follow your will, Amen.

After that a devotee can recite any small chapter of the Koran. Many recite ch.112 which bears the title "unity" and is worded as follows: "Say, God is one. He is eternal. He never breeds anybody nor is he bred by anybody. There is nobody equal to him." He completes that second gesture with the words "Allahu Akbar, the only God is Allah".

In the third gesture too he is standing but this time he is bent into two. Legs are straight. Hands are on the knees. Bending so, he says three times: "Glory to God the most high". Saying that, the devotee straightens himself.

In the fourth gesture, very much like in the second, keeping his hands on the belly, he stands straight and says the following words: "God listens to the one who thanks and praises God. Lord, may you be praised."

The fifth gesture is one of falling down in prostration. The forehead is on the ground. The hands too are on the ground but what touch the floor are only the palms. The elbow should not touch the floor. The toes of the legs are bent forward. Staying so, he says three times "Allahu Akbar, The only God is Allah".

In the sixth or final gesture, the devotee straightens himself up and then sits down on the hind part of his legs. The hands are on the legs close to the knees. Sitting so, he says "Forgive me Lord and have mercy on me." After that, as in the fifth gesture, he prostrates himself on the ground and resumes at once the standing position. This brings one "Rakah" or prayer-round to an end.

Thereafter the "Rakahs" are repeated according to the number required. This prayer-exercise could be done at home or wherever one is, but if there is a mosque close by, he can do it in it along with others. But going to the mosque is considered essential only for the noon-prayer on Friday. At the noon prayer on Fridays a sermon is preached. Friday is the week's sacred day for the Muslims just as Sunday is for the Christians and Saturday for the Jews. But Friday is a public holiday only in Pakistan.

The Mosque: In every area inhabited by Muslims, there is a mosque. A mosque is usually built of stone or brick in the form of a square with an open hall in the center. Minarets or slender towers rise in front or at the corners. Beside the minarets are balconies from which the Muezzin or the caller-to-prayer makes his announcements. The wall that faces Mecca contains a semi-circled niche (Mihrab). Devotees do their prayer exercise in front of that.

To the right of the niche is a pulpit from which the preacher (Khatib) delivers the sermon. The courtyard may contain a tank or taps for ritual washings before prayer. Mosques have no images and paintings, but walls, pillars and ceilings are decorated with verses from the Koran in Arabic script. When the Salat prayer-exercise is done in the mosque, devotees stay in clear-cut rows. At the end of the exercise everyone greets first the one on the left and then the one on the right saying "May the peace and mercy of Allah be with you."

82. Almsgiving (Zakat)

Almsgiving is an important duty that a Muslim has to fulfill throughout the year. Every Muslim has to set aside a part of his income to offer to the poor and the needy such as widows, orphans, poor and sick. According to the Koran 40% of one's income should be donated for charitable activity. From the income of grain and fruit produced in lands endowed with water facilities 10% should be given. From the profits received by supplying water 20% should be given.

By doing so, a Muslim believes that he shares with his brethren what he has been given by God. In the words attributed to God in the Koran, "Among my creatures, the most valuable treasure is the merciful person who gives alms to the needy".

83. The Month-long Fast of Ramadan (Sawm)

The fourth important duty of a Muslim is the observance of fast during the month of Ramadan (Ramazan). The word for "fasting" in Arabic is "Sawm". Ramadan is the ninth month in the Muslim calendar which is different from the regular calendar. Since the Muslim months are calculated according to the movements of the moon, the number of days for a month may vary from 27 to 30. All Muslim adults, except those who are infirm, are bound to observe the fast.

The fast begins at dawn and lasts the whole day until sundown. Food can be taken before the start of the fast. But during the time of the fast no food or drink can be taken. At the end of each day's fast the common custom is to take three dates and to drink water saying "Lord Allah, I have engaged in the fast for your glory. Now with the food provided by you, I close the fast."

During the month of the fast a significant place is given to acts of charity to the poor and the needy. The month-long fast ends with the "festival of breaking the fast" called "Id-al Fitr". That is considered one of the main festivals of the Muslims. On that day all go to the mosque for the midday service.

84. The Pilgrimage (Hajj)

The fifth duty of a Muslim is going on pilgrimage to Mecca at least once in a life time. But the duty is binding only on those who have the health and the financial means to do so.

The pilgrimage is usually performed during the 12th month of the Muslim calendar called "Hajj". For many people in regions remote from Arabia, the Hajj is the climax of years of yearning and some make it more than once. Upon entering the sacred area of Mecca, pilgrims don a special dress and after completing the ceremony have their heads shaved.

The full ceremony of the Hajj is quite elaborate and requires several days but its principal part is the circum-ambulation of the Ka'aba. The pilgrims must run round the shrine seven times, three times rather fast and the rest of the times slowly. Every time they pass the black stone they kiss it or at least touch it. Everybody who completes the pilgrimage acquires the honorific title of "Hajj" or "Haji".

Those are the officially recognized Five Pillars of Islam. But some preachers add to them a sixth called "Holy War" or "Jihad". The Holy War is a concept that has been more or less natural to religions taken in their politicized form.

Such religions consider as justifiable the concept of "Conquer nations and Convert the inhabitants". In Christianity "Holy Wars" were called "Crusades". But today Muslim mystics and Sufis maintain that the true Jihad is against sin within oneself.

85. The Formative Value of the Pillars

The brief explanation of the Five Pillars given above should be sufficient to make students of religion (particularly if they are non-Muslims) aware of the primary duties that every Muslim has obligatorily to fulfill. But if they are to understand the purpose and the practical value of the Pillars, they should try to get at least a rough idea of the intentions that Muhammad would have had in composing and imposing them. This is because, if not for those Pillars, Islam would not be what it is today.

The Pillars have given Islam a socio-religious culture of a unique nature, – one which has made it different from almost all other religions. Therefore, it would be normal for anybody to conclude that

Muhammad has composed the Pillars with great insight and with the vision of a version of religion all his own.

But to analyze the mind of another, particularly if it is of an extra-ordinary person like the founder of a world-wide religion, is no easy matter. All that we could do is to take rather haphazardly some constituent elements of the Pillars, and try to guess why he would have included them. Being just suspicions, and not part of officially approved Muslim Theology, the points mentioned here should be taken only for what they are worth.

As an example, we could first select the technique that Muhammad devised to get the times for worship announced to the devotees. He created for it a method, altogether novel. He got someone from the mosque to shout out the right time for each exercise of worship. One could say that, at a time when time-indicating clocks were not available in houses, this was an understandable solution.

But the call was not just an announcement for indicating the time. It was a well-thought out technique to prevent anybody from shirking the duty after hearing the announcement. There was a psychological pressure attached to the call. When the announcement came there was nothing anybody could do than obey and engage in worship. Being, by his very nature a commander, Muhammad would not leave room for any of his orders to be left undone. The method has now lasted for centuries and even in this technologically developed world, no one has found a better method to replace it.

Another similar element of the Pillars that could be given thought is the ritual of ablution that devotees had to perform before engaging in worship. Cleansing of oneself with water before worship is recommended in all religions. But Muhammad did not stop with just a recommendation. He made it an obligatory matter and presented in detail how the washing had to be done. He made precise how the palms, the ears, the nostrils, the face, head and legs were to be washed and the number of times they were to be done.

Muhammad knew that the tribal folk of Arabia living in the desert and without much water were not prone to cleanliness and sanitary habits. Very likely what made him impose this somewhat arduous exercise was his desire to ensure that the community of his followers was physically clean and healthy.

Then we can take the pattern of worship he prescribed for his devotees. That pattern could indicate not just one but two vital aspects of his thought pattern. On one side, Muhammad is the only religious leader who went to the extent of prescribing as many as five times of prayer per day. At each step of the prayer round, the devotee had to proclaim "There is no other God but Allah". Probably his intention in getting his followers to repeat that refrain so many times is to make sure that polytheism that was widely spread in the surroundings was totally wiped out of his community. He wanted to make Islam the religion in which monotheism was professed in its boldest, simplest and clearest form.

There is also a second side to the pattern of worship he wanted followed. He did not consider prayer or worship purely a mental matter. For him prayer had both a mind-building and body-building side to it. For Muhammad, prayer was a series of exercises consisting of actions, like standing, sitting, bending and prostrating. Taken together the Muslim prayer or Salat is like the mind and body building drills that military personnel are expected to perform in their training. Muhammad was a disciplinarian, and he wanted discipline, uniform behavior and bodily health to be qualities of each and every Muslim in the whole world.

The two aspects of the Muslim form of worship could show two sides of Muhammad's life. On one side, he was a visionary religious leader. He wanted to make monotheism the very essence of religion. He upheld that submission to the will of Almighty God or, in other words, respect to the right values of life, is what made any human being internally perfect. On the other side, Muhammad was a far-sighted society builder and, judging from the number of wars he won during his life time, an astute military leader. The month-long fast that Muhammad prescribed for all adults has the same educative purpose. All Muslims going without food during daytime for as long a time as a month cannot but result in the community being highly disciplined and highly united.

The fifth Pillar of Islam or the obligation for all Muslims to visit Mecca once in their life time is still another point that could be given consideration. It is an exercise that would astound any non-Muslim. It is true that only those who are in good health and have the financial means for it are bound to fulfill it. But the decision of Muhammad to impose the obligation on Muslims not just of Arabia or of nearby areas, but of the entire world is a bold one. No one would have thought it even realizable. But history shows that the decree has been carried out for centuries. Muhammad wanted Muslims to enjoy their religion and be proud of their religion. People from all over the world gathering together in one place contributed to the feeling of close fellowship and deep union among Muslims. All such prescriptions show what a far sighted society-organizer and religion-builder Muhammad was.

86. Islam Today

However high be the level of unity and uniformity that the Five Pillars have built up in the Muslim community, we cannot deny that there are many politically split divisions too in Islam. Of these, the two most prominent are the "Sunni" and the "Shia". The bigger group is the "Sunni". Since the word "Sunna" means "original tradition", they consider themselves the more orthodox group. They consist of nearly 80 % of the total Muslim population. The biggest group after the "Sunni" is the "Shia".

We cannot deny that the groups so divided are often in political conflict with one another. Such conflicts are inevitable in religious communities of the politicized form. But even with such splits and differences, Islam has been able to safeguard to a great extent its uniformity in forms of worship.

Among the different religions of today, Islam could be said to be the one that has expanded the fastest in the world. Early in the 7th century, unnoticed by the rest of the world, Islam started in the interior of Arabia, and within an amazingly short time, – a little more than 20 years – it gathered momentum and absorbed the unruly tribesmen of the peninsula.

Spilling out from Arabia it rapidly extended political sway over the surrounding regions, consolidated its hold in the years that followed, and in the third century of its existence developed a most brilliant and creative culture. Its advent changed the course of history and enriched human heritage by the creation of an illustrious civilization. Today it continues to be the spiritual anchor and guide to a major portion of humanity.

**World Religions
Part Five
Two Forms of Any Religion**

Chapter 1
Two Senses of Word "Religion"

There was a time when no questions were raised about the way a religion had to be practiced. Every religion was practiced in the way the believer was taught to from the time of birth.

But today we cannot look at religion in as simple a way as that. Too many conflicts taking place both in society and in the minds of individuals seem rather strangely to have their source in religion. In many parts of the world, people of different religious traditions wage war with one another. Then most religions are divided and composed of denominations that are at logger-heads with each other. Religion has problems with science too. Often religion discards scientific views and science takes religious teachings as myths. Nor do religion and politics get on well together. The enmity between political leaders and religious authorities is such that in certain areas practice of religion is forbidden by the state. Then, what is more pathetic still, we have instances where devoted followers of a religion cannot in conscience submit to what their religious teachers declare as right and wrong.

Amidst such situations, it is not surprising if people ask questions such as these which are not easy to answer: Is the religion which is behind such conflicts identical with the one which is said to make people holy, sublime and even divine? Is religion a unifier of humanity or its divider? Does religion enlighten people or blind them? There is only one answer possible. There is an ambiguity in the word "religion" as used today.

It is consoling to know that many scholars of religion today are aware of this perplexity and are looking for solutions to it. According to some, the best solution is to "drop" the word altogether and never to use it in discussions on religion. One such is Wilfred Cantwell Smith who in his book "The Meaning and End of Religion" says:

The word "religion" has had many meanings. It would be better dropped. This is partly because of its ambiguity and partly because most of its traditional meanings on scrutiny are illegitimate.[1]

The suggestion to drop the word may not be actually workable, but the drastic nature of the proposal should make one realize what confusion and misunderstanding the word causes. That suggestion

---

[1] Wilfred Cantwell Smith, *The Meaning and End of Religion* (London, SPCK, 1978) p.198

alone is enough to show why a serious reflection on the word "religion" is indispensable in any study on religion.

The new view that I want to bring out here as a solution to the problem of ambiguity is basically that the word "religion" can be understood in two irreconcilably distinct senses. The complexity comes from the fact that the two senses are not correctly distinguished when the word "religion" is used.

87. Religion, Born-to

Of the two ways of understanding religion the one of which the boundaries are easy to demarcate and so, easier to talk about, is brought out in the dialogue given below. This dialogue which we have taken from a course in the Sociology of Religion is imaginatively presented as taking place between a teacher and pupil in a French school.

Catherine, what is your nationality? My nationality is French. What is your religion? My religion is Christianity.

Catherine, what would your nationality have been, if you had been born in Tibet? If I had been born in Tibet, my nationality would have been Tibetan. What would your religion have been, if you had been born in Tibet? If I had been born in Tibet, my religion would, very likely, have been Buddhism.

Catherine, what would your nationality have been, if you had been born in Saudi Arabia? If I had been born in Saudi Arabia, my nationality would have been Saudi Arabian. If you had been born in Saudi Arabia, what would your religion have been? If I had been born in Saudi Arabia, very likely my religion would have been Islam.

Catherine, what would your nationality have been if you had been born in India? If I had been born in India, my nationality would have been Indian. If you had been born in India, what would your religion have been? If I had been born in India, my religion would, very likely, have been Hinduism.

If so Catherine, isn't it by chance that you and I are Christian and French? Isn't it in the same way that all people acquire their nationality and religion? If things are so, does it not imply that we who, as French people, are today upholding the supremacy of Christianity, would have been upholding the supremacy of quite another religion had we been born elsewhere? Does that not mean that we should re-examine our customary attitude to nationality and religion, whether of our own, or of others?

This dialogue has no doubt a hurting side to it. Its composer seems to have wanted to drum into his students a truth that many of us would prefer to see just left buried underground. It is not easy to muster the honesty and the humility necessary to look fearlessly at the roots of our religious affiliations. The fact is that the religion we take pride in adhering to, and usually hail as the best religion in the world, is one that each of us has got as accidentally as the color of our skin.

I am Catholic, Protestant, Hindu, Buddhist or Muslim simply because my parents were so. My religion is not something I have freely and conscientiously chosen. Before seeking membership in it, I did not submit it to any examination. I didn't weigh the pros and cons of its values. I was just born to it. This "born-to" form of religion is what most people speak of proudly as "our religion" and want established in the world as the only true religion.

An important point to be noted here is that the religion acquired at birth is not any religion but that of the parents. The religion of the parents being that of their ancestors, religion that is inherited is always that of the clan. Inherited religion is different from clan to clan in the same way as inherited language called the "mother-tongue" is different from clan to clan. Each clan has a religion of its own just as it has a mother-tongue of its own. In any clan both language and religion are the same as those of their ancestors. Religion as much as language is what convinces the members of any particular community that they are inseparably united in heart and that as a group their solidarity is unbreakable. This is what leads to the popular assumption that religion of the inherited form will never be able to be done away with.

88. Religion, Awakened-to

Inherited religion, however, is not the only reality to which the word "religion" is applied today. It is also applied to the one which one enters after becoming mature enough to seek the meaning of life and look for a way to bring it to its fulfillment. The great founders of religions were concerned mainly about that adult form of religion. Religion as they understood it calls for reflection, judgment, decision. What that type of religion stands for becomes clear if we take a glance at the lives and teachings of just the Buddha, Jesus and Muhammad.

Two Senses of Word "Religion"

Siddhartha Gautama, who eventually became the Buddha, started at the age of 29 to search for the religion that he wanted for himself. When he did not find it in the schools of asceticism and meditation that he frequented, he looked for it on his own. When, at the age of 35, he actually found it, he referred to that moment of discovery as the "enlightenment" or the "awakening of the mind". It was at that moment that he awakened to the reality of life and to the path that leads to genuine happiness.

Ever after, the Buddha ("the awakened") preached that religion of "mind-awakening" (Buddhism) to those around him. His mission was to awaken people from the dormant state of their minds. That religion of the "awakened to" form is not one that a person can inherit or acquire at birth.

Jesus of Nazareth did not practice or preach what we called above the "born-to" type of religion. He referred to his form of religion as the one to which a person is "re-born". When Nicodemus came to him to find out from him the path to the Kingdom of God, Jesus wanted him to be "re-born". Taking the word literally, Nicodemus queried:

"But how is it possible for a man to be re-born when he is old? Can he enter his mother's womb a second time and be born?"

The answer of Jesus throws light on what we are to understand by religion of the "awakened-to" or the "reborn-to" form. He said:

"Flesh can give birth only to flesh. It is Spirit that gives birth to spirit".[2]

Muhammad the Founder of Islam discovered what religion was only at the age of forty when he was meditating in a cave. He was then a married person too. In the course of his meditations he saw that real religion was submission to the laws laid down by the Supreme Being whom he called Allah. In the Koran his awakening is attributed to a revelation by an angel from heaven.

For quite some time scholars have conducted researches to find out how religions came to exist and what they actually do to people. Among them there are two who have something very powerful to say about the issue we are concerned with, namely, the two forms of religion.

---

[2] John 3: 1-8

89. View of Emile Durkheim

One is the eminent sociologist of religion Emile Durkheim (1858-1917). As can be seen from his book "Elementary Forms of Religious Experience"[3] Durkheim was strongly of the opinion that religion was a constituent element of the common pattern of life of clan-communities. According to him religions are there to ensure the unity and the solidarity of clan-communities.

An idea of Durkheim which is typical of his sociological thought is that religion has nothing more to it than what is contained in the concept of clan-community. But, of course, we must not forget that for him a clan was not just an agglomeration of individuals. Members were inter-related and the sense of affinity which this produced transformed the community into one moral body. In the way he implied, a clan community was one body because it was animated by one soul.

To designate that moral body he used the Judeo-Christian term "church". For him, religion was just "church" or an association in which members had a reason to feel inter-related. The code of beliefs and practices that the "church" upheld had no other purpose than to keep the community-group bound together and to give it an identity of its own. He put so much stress on the clan-community that he explained even the belief in God as an outcome of an individual's submission to the community.

"In fact, we can say that the believer is not deceived when he believes in the existence of a moral power upon which he depends and from which he receives all that is best in himself. This power exists. It is society".[4]

What Durkheim tries to bring out is the side of life that we comprehend with our physical senses. According to him an individual's life was bred by the parent and protected by the parental community. No individual can grow up physically and mentally and achieve the goals of his life without the support of the community he belongs to. In very brief, the real life-giver, life maintainer, and life developer of any human being is not any entity outside society but the society itself that he belongs to. As he worded it,

---

[3] Emile Durkheim, *Elementary Forms of Religious Experience: A Study in Religious Sociology* (George Allen & Unwin, New York, 1915)

[4] ibid. p.257

"In a general way, it is unquestionable that a society has all that is necessary to arouse the sensation of the divine in minds merely by the power it has over them. For to its members, it is what a god is to his worshipers".[5]

Durkheim focused attention exclusively on one form of religion, namely, the one we have referred to as the "born-to" form. He overlooked completely that of the "reborn-to" or the "awakened-to". But to understand the problems and complications of religion in modern society, Durkheim's view regarding the clan-group and its hold on the religious behavior of individuals is invaluable.

90. View of Rudolf Otto

The other authority whose views are fundamental for the issue in question is Rudolf Otto (1869-1937). He concentrated on the other version of religion. Judging from his book "The Idea of the Holy"[6] he understood the power behind the origin and sustenance of life in a way different from that of Durkheim. For Otto, life of any form originated from a supreme source of Divine Power and depended on that Power for its survival and development. Since this mysterious Power exceeds the grasp of the senses, in different religions it has been portrayed through different symbols and pictures. In the Judeo-Christian tradition it has been portrayed as an entity with almighty power. Even though the reality is verbally inexpressible, the conscience or the inner sight of any human being has an uncontroversial vision of it.

Because of his close awareness of the Hindu-Buddhist religious systems of India in which the concept of God is different from that of the Judeo-Christian tradition, Rudolf Otto abstained from describing the source of religion as "God-consciousness". He referred to it broadly as just "numinous consciousness"[7] an expression close in meaning to "the sense of the Sacred" or the "sense of the Sacred Source of Existence". According to him that consciousness of the "Sacred" is the basis of all religion. As he said:

---

[5] ibid. p.236-237

[6] Rudolf Otto, *The Idea of the Holy* (Oxford University Press, England, 1923)

[7] ibid. p.6

"There is no religion in which it does not live as the real inmost core; and without it no religion would be worthy of the name".[8]

For Rudolf Otto religion is not, as for Durkheim, a form of "church" or "a united uniform community" but a matter of "personal spiritual development". For any human being born as an infant in an extremely weak state of body and mind, to grow up to a point at which he can discern between what is right and what is wrong takes time. From there to acquire the mental maturity to do always only what is right and avoid what is wrong is not easy. For that divine assistance is necessary. Achievement of humanness in its perfect form makes a person divine. It is also what is called "salvation" in the deeper sense of the word. By keeping united with the Divine Spirit any human being, irrespective of color, caste or creed, can achieve spiritual salvation on earth corporeally and beyond earth incorporeally.

Here again we have to say of Rudolf Otto what we said of Emile Durkheim. He too focused attention on just one sense of the word, the one we referred to as "religion re-born-to" or "religion awakened-to". As an insightful exponent of that spiritual form of religion, we cannot think of a better person than Rudolf Otto.

As will be evident to anybody, the disparity between the interpretations of these two scholars is by no means small. For Durkheim, religion is purely a clan matter and its purpose is safeguarding the cultural unity of the clan. There will therefore be as many religions as there are such culturally distinct communities. The teacher-pupil dialogue cited above is thus quite in keeping with his view of religion. For the French, the Saudi Arabians, the Indians and the Tibetans to have religions that distinguish them from one another is just normal.

For Rudolf Otto, on the contrary, religion is purely a spiritual matter. It is what helps a person, to arrive at his or her highest stature as a human being and be divine. The aspiration to be human at its divine level is the same in the Frenchman and the Tibetan as also in the Hindu and the Muslim.

What could be really disturbing however, is the question that one is compelled to ask here: If scholars as great as these can take the word "religion" in two different senses, is it a matter for surprise if ordinary people mix up the senses when they use it? Is anyone to

---

[8] ibid. p.169

blame if at one time people wage wars under the name of "religion" and at the other engage in activities that promote peace and harmony?

If to avoid confusion we are to give each of them a name, we could call the one Emile Durkheim gave prominence to as "Cultural religion". This is because religion is an integral part of the culture of any community that is racially and regionally distinct. The one Rudolf Otto gave prominence to could very simply be called "Spiritual religion". This is because to live spiritually is to live according to the sublime values of the verbally inexpressible inner spirit that every human being is endowed with. What we need to remember here is that any religion with a given name can be practiced as also propagated in either a cultural or a spiritual way.

Chapter 2
Cultural Religion, Spiritual Religion

In contemporary society, there is probably no topic so much subjected to discussion as religion. But it is seriously to be doubted if the discussions yield the intended results. The main reason for it is that most discussions are led by individuals who do not take seriously into account the distinction between cultural religion and spiritual religion.

91. Cultural Religion – Inherited by Birth

To understand clearly what cultural religion is we must go back to the earliest days of human history when tribes lived apart from each other, and each tribe had a distinct culture with a religion of its own. All the members of the clan shared a) one ancestral history, b) one geographical habitation or motherland, c) one common language called the "mother-tongue", d) one common source of economic sustenance, e) one political chief, and last but not least, f) one religion with one fixed set of beliefs, artistic symbols, rituals, and behavioral rules. Being part of culture, the role of religion was to provide the clan with an identity which made it distinct from other clans.

Two examples of such culturally religious communities are Judaism and Hinduism. The two religions belong to two long-standing clan-communities of our time, the Jews and the Indians. A characteristic feature of those two age-old clan-communities is that their religions have no proper names. The name of the religion is the very name of the clan. The word "Jew" points to membership in both a clan and a religion. The word "Hindu" and "Indian" are interconnected. To be "Indian" is to be "Hindu". The only difference between these two groups is that the Jewish sense of clan-community comes from the oneness of their ancestry and that of the Hindus from the oneness of the region they inhabit, namely, the "Indus" valley.

Both these religions are endowed with a voluminous scripture coming down from early times. The scripture of the Jews is called the "Bible" and that of the Hindus the "Vedas". But what is important to remember here is that both the Bible and the Vedas contain not only clan-protective or clan-perpetuating traditions for the members to follow uniformly, but also values that individual members should adhere to for becoming spiritually sublime. But unfortunately what is given priority to by the masses and the religious authorities is the former. The second is relegated to the attention of just those believers who are in search of right life-values.

92. Major Religions and Culture

Such uni-cultural ancient religions are not very different from the multi-cultural modern religions that we today call "major religions". The best known among them are Buddhism, Christianity and Islam. Hinduism too could be included in the category, since in recent times it has begun to spread in Western countries.

The multi-culturalness of the major religions is a matter that has to be approached with great discernment as appearances can be deceptive. There are two factors to be given consideration to. First, major religions are not as uniform as they are imagined to be. According to the impression created, Hinduism, Buddhism, Christianity and Islam are religions with one fixed form. But that is not so.

In reality, there are many Hinduisms, Buddhisms, Christianities and Islams. Buddhism of Tibet, for example, is different from Buddhism of Japan, and Buddhism of Japan from that of Sri Lanka. Christianity is the same. The Greek Orthodox, the Roman Catholic, Protestant and the post-Protestant versions of Christianity are vastly different from each other.

When one particular religion is found in such diverse forms, we naturally ask what the cause of such diversities and even divisions could be. Is it possible that all these forms have been invented and initiated by the same founder? Could it be that both the Theravada and the Mahayana forms of Buddhism were initiated by the same Buddha, and that the Catholic, Orthodox Protestant and post-Protestant versions of Christianity were started by the same Jesus?

There is no doubt that the religious thought of the great visionaries, in spite of the fact that they themselves lived in fixed cultures, was supra-cultural and so universal. But as soon as their thought was accepted by a clan or national body, it was adopted to fit the shape of its age-old culture.

Second, we must not forget that inherited religions do not always remain uni-racial. This is because one race can conquer other races and become an empire. In an empire the governing race imposes its religion on all sub-races. Missionaries have generally come out of empire-shaped religions. They have diffused not only the spirituality of the religion but also the culture of the empire.

Every major or empire-extended religion is rooted in a culture, – one that could be treated as its mother-culture. That of Christianity is European culture; of Islam, Arab. Those mother-cultures have thereafter acted as molds reshaping the cultures of the nations into which the religion was introduced. With regard to Christianity, it was in that Roman (eventually European) shape that Christianity was later diffused in the rest of the world. The vestments worn by the Catholic priest at ceremonies have little to do with Jesus Christ. This is no less true of other religions.

The very tendency of religions to lean on the mother-tongue of their earliest ancestors, – Hebrew and Greek in Judaism, Latin and Greek in Christianity, Arabic in Islam, Sanskrit in Hinduism, Pali and Sanskrit in Buddhism, – has the same basis.

93. Religion as Tradition

For culturally-linked communities, whether uni-racial or multi-racial, religion is basically a tradition to be handed down from generation to generation. The tradition's aim is to keep the clan's past, present and future generations united together as one large family.

Below is a picture that could be of help to visualize in a general way what religions – even major religions – are when taken in their clan-protective form.

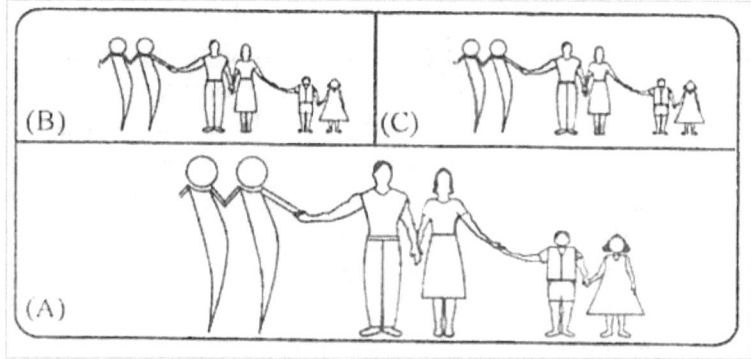

The three boxes in the picture portray followers of three different religions. The difference in their beliefs and rites is not indicated here. But the boxes show that, however different they are in beliefs and rites, all the three religions, here named A, B, C, have one main function to perform, namely, to keep the clan united together. In each box three generations, the past, the present and the future are

shown holding hands together to show that they belong to one clan and derive from one ancestry. What the three boxes intend to impress is that religion is different from religion, because clan is different from clan.

The picture is sufficient to show what happens even to major religions when taken in the clan-protective form. Then Hinduism becomes the religion of the Indian or Indianized community, Christianity of the European or Europeanized community, and Islam of the Arabian or Arabianized community.

94. Spiritual Religion — A Way of Right Living

Rather paradoxically however, humanness is not something that people acquire at birth or by the simple fact that they are endowed with a human form. People are born only with the potential to be human. That is how the achievement of humanness at its perfect level becomes the ultimate goal of human beings.

The elevation of the individual from the "not fully human" to the "fully human" is what is referred to as "salvation" of the spiritual form. This should not be confused with salvation or liberation of the cultural form. If we take an example from the Bible, what Moses achieved by making the Israelites escape from the tyrannical control of the Pharaohs of Egypt was cultural or political liberation. Many today are at a loss to comprehend what salvation of the spiritual form implies. One reason for it is that the redemption brought about by religion is not of the physically visible body, but of the invisible mind. It is hardly possible for anybody to distinguish a mentally liberated person from a non-liberated one. Externally they will be the same. A saint and a criminal are not different in their facial features.

A rough sketch could be useful here to indicate what religious liberation of the spiritual form involves. If presented schematically, the physical form of the human being as seen by sight and the two levels of the inner personality as seen by insight would be as follows:

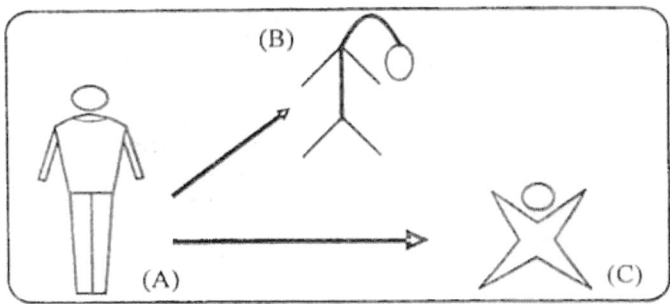

A) Human being as seen by physical sight.
B) View of the inner personality at the mentally disoriented level. The "self" of this level is bent on itself and so, deformed. It is of a skeletal nature.
C) Insight view of the inner personality at the adult level. It is representative of human-hood in its completely liberated form and of the mind in its rightly oriented divinized form.

Of the numerous explanations given to religious liberation, the one that a modern person will find easy to comprehend is that given by the Buddha. For him the liberation that human beings needed most, was from the stunted state of their minds as this is what brought pain and anxiety to people.

The human mind in its initial unenlightened state is controlled by emotional desires. In that state, individuals fail to see what brings them true peace and joy. They cannot understand that true self-fulfillment comes on one side, from a life of self-less submission to the dictates of one's inner conscience, and on the other, from a life of selfless care and concern for the helpless and the needy of any caste or creed. Due to that lack of understanding they run after sleazy objects of enjoyment which ultimately bring them more sorrow than contentment. That is why the Buddha made "right view or vision of life" the basis of his path to liberation. The Buddha's explanation makes it very clear that liberation is a matter which pertains to the realm of the enlightened mind or of the mind at its spiritual level. For him, the role of religion is to help people pass from mental immaturity to mental maturity.

Chapter 3
Two Ways of Practicing and Propagating Any Religion

If as explained above, any religion, such as Hinduism, Buddhism, Judaism, Christianity and Islam can be conceived of in either a cultural or a spiritual way, it goes without saying that any of them will be able to be practiced and propagated in either of those two ways.

95. Cultural Christian and Spiritual Christian

For purpose of illustration we can take two Frenchmen who like most Frenchmen are both Roman Catholic. The first we can call the "Culturally Catholic Frenchman" or in short "Cultural Frenchman" and the other the "Spiritually Catholic Frenchman" or in short the "Spiritual Frenchman". The Cultural Frenchman's aim is to be a good French Catholic. His conviction is that the French race is the best race in the world, and Roman Catholicism, the only true religion. People of all other religions are "pagans", a word meaning "uncivilized heathens". Pagans are not entitled to "salvation".

He accepts as God's word the sacred texts of his religion, the Bible. For him no symbolical or mythological language is used in it. Everything in the Bible is to be understood literally. Therefore he accepts as unquestionable historic facts that God created the world in seven days, and that Jesus was born of a virgin. He has his own interpretation of "Church", "conversion" and "missionary work". What missionaries have to do is to make people of other religions or denominations give up their institution and enroll in the Roman Catholic Church governed by the Pope in the Vatican.

The spiritual Frenchman is different. But the difference is not externally visible, since he too engages in the same religious exercises as the other. He celebrates the same festivals. He too respects the Bible. But his interpretation of it is different. What he takes as revealed by God is not the legendary external story but the deeper meaning beneath it.

According to him what the Creation story teaches is not that the universe was produced in seven days but that there is a humanly incomprehensible mysterious wisdom behind everything that exists or happens in the universe. What the virginal birth of Jesus implies is that the teachings of Jesus were so extraordinary, that it is better to attribute their source to a divine father than his earthly carpenter father. Further for him what missionaries have to do is not to make people give up their earlier religion and join Catholicism but to make them pass from their un-liberated selfish state of mind to a liberated selfless one.

But what makes him most different from the cultural Frenchman is in the all-inclusive way he looks at life. He is a person who in his understanding of life does not leave out the thought of death. Death no doubt has something strange about it. There is nobody who does not know that death is inevitable, but there is also nobody who wouldn't wish that it did not come his way. The uncanny side of death comes from the sorrow that relatives feel at the loss of someone dear to them.

But to the dying person death is a joyful reality. If detached from ailments that precede it, by itself death is not painful or fearful. Death is the sacred moment at which a person after his corporeal existence on earth rejoins incorporeally with the supreme source of his life, the Divine Sprit, to live in spiritual bliss ever after. Anyone who looks forward to death always prepares for it. The best preparation for death and for living with peace of mind on earth, is to keep united in heart with the immortal Divine Spirit while giving prominence in one's day to day life to the practice of care and concern for others.

On another side the thought of death makes him accept all human beings irrespective of creed, color or caste as his equals. He knows that birth makes people racially different and death makes them humanly equal. What makes the spiritual Frenchman so different from the cultural Frenchman is beyond doubt the primacy he gives to the thought of his own death.

96. Purpose of the Book

As we come to the end of our book, there could be readers who would want to ask what the purpose of the book is, and if it has anything new to offer to students of religion. There is of course no doubt that this is far from being a comprehensive book on world's religions. Of the hundreds of religions prevailing in the world today, it deals with only five and they too are treated very briefly.

But still this book is one meant for use as a preliminary text for anybody who wants to get an idea of the world's religions and of religion in general. That is because it is a book with a novel aim. That aim is to make people learn of religions in a way they could respect the religions of others. The most effective way to make people respect other religions, and also bring people of different religions closer to one another is to convince them that all religions consist of two forms, one cultural and the other spiritual. Taken from the cultural side, all religions, – whether Hinduism, Buddhism, Judaism, Christianity, Islam or any other – are different from each other and will be different for ever. But from the spiritual side, the aspirations of the followers of different religions – whether Hinduism, Buddhism, Judaism, Christianity, Islam or any other – have much in common.

When the common aspirations are taken into account anyone will see that however different cultural religions are in their beliefs and rites, followers of all religions are all simple human beings struggling to pass from their transient and sorrowful state of life to a permanent and peaceful one. However diversely different groups of believers may word it, salvation of the spiritual form, or eternal peace of mind achieved through unity with the indefinable divine source of life, is universal and open to everybody. If so, people of all religions seeking salvation have to be treated as brothers and sisters of one spiritually uniform family.

A second aspect, in which this book could be considered new, is the type of language used in it. As everybody knows no religion can avoid resorting to legend and myth because it has often to deal with intangible spiritual matters inexpressible through day-to-day earthly terms. Further mythical expressions of one religion are different from those of others and so are un-intelligible to followers of other religions. That un-intelligibility is what makes people of one religion often look down on other religions and even show an aversion to them.

What this book attempts to do is to replace the mythical language common to all religions with the home-spoken secular language that anybody is at ease with. But of course the secularization of the mythical language has to be done in such a way that the deep spiritual lessons illustrated by the myths are not distorted but made to come out more clearly. That is what I have tried to do to the best of my ability.

97. A Matter for Theologians of All Religions

This book which has attempted to present religion in a way that promotes inter human amity and better inter-religious understanding could be incomplete if it does not attempt to awaken theologians of all religions to a need that they may have to fulfill in the future.

As would be clear from what has been said in this book, every religion today has an institutional theology (or an unchangeable set of beliefs, rituals and code of conduct) of its own. This theology makes any religion different from all others.

But for the building up of a united humanity, the world may need in the future a spiritual theology acceptable to all institutional religions and which focuses attention on the common root and ultimate goal of all religions. Such a theology will have to expound the reality of life after birth and life after death that all religions are in agreement with and which all human beings are subconsciously convinced of.

It is our sincere hope that, even in a small way, this book will incite theologians of different religions, while retaining their inherited institutional theology to the extent needed by their communities, to develop in their own way a spiritual theology or (if expressible in one newly-coined term) "spirituology" that people of all religions will be at home with. If that happens, there is no doubt that the world we live in, will soon be a place inhabited by people who, however racially and religiously distinct by birth, will be uniformly aspiring for greater spiritual nobility.

About iPubCloud.com

iPubCloud.com is privileged and proud to be your wisdom resource, and perhaps even your publisher. Focusing on globally transformative books by authors from across the world, we showcase creative thinkers and writers who influence us in matters of Equality-Unity, Deep Dialogue-Critical Thinking, and Planet Sustainability. Scholarly works are essential in the development of all creative minds including children and teens—and yes, producing visions, dreams, and escape for all of us!

You will discover continually-curated book lists such as those culled from the New York Times, Amazon reader reviews, prestigious library recommendations, and iPubCloud subject matter advisors.

You may relax knowing you, your children, family, friends, and associates are in excellent hands. iPubCloud has extended its commitment to excellence assuring your financial confidentiality and security by contracting with the globally-recognized fulfillment company, Amazon.

Everything you order will be delivered by Amazon. Better yet, for your convenience, we've extended our agreement. Now, not only will you receive iPub author's original works, you will also have access to everything Amazon makes available on a global basis.

From pet food to your baby's favorite dream toy; from fine clothing for special events to the computer you have wished for; you'll find it at iPubCloud.com. Order everything you need and all that you wish for conveniently through your Internet Pub.

Remember, this is *your* Internet Pub, so connect with friends and have fruitful discussions together. Together we can identify and make the changes required for us all--our families, business associates, and friends to create a better world.

Connect with us on Facebook by going to *https://www.facebook.com/iPubCloud/*. Have something to say? Submit it to our blog *https://www.ipubcloud.com/blog/* and join our email list info@ipubcloud.com.

Remember, *don't keep us a secret.*

iPub Global Connection, LLC
www.iPubCloud.com
550 W. Baseline Rd., #303
Mesa, AZ 85210
info@iPubCloud.com